# Growing Up Isn't All Fishing and Hunting

## By

## Leon "Buckshot" Anderson

ISBN: 1-4107-0381-9 (e-book)
ISBN: 1-4107-0382-7 (Paperback)

This book is printed on acid free paper.

1stBooks - rev. 01/10/03

# Dedication

I sincerely dedicate these vivid, memorable, memories of my youth to my parents, "Mom & Dad Anderson", (better known as Andy and Esther) who, with their outstanding guidance, love and caring, also had the wisdom to "let me be a boy". Even though,...

"GROWING UP ISN'T ALL FISHING AND HUNTING!"

# Table of Contents

# Forward

The path from birth to maturity is never straight, nor clear. And the path will most certainly be twisting! One will find many forks in the path of life, and sometimes just plain luck will allow one to select the correct route. However, most of the time one's good sense (or possibly the lack of it) will be the deciding factor in choosing the correct fork.

Having parents, relatives, friends and teachers who assist in laying the groundwork for making positive choices is probably the best aid in helping one choose the "right path".

I was very fortunate to have all four!

Enjoy my journey!

# Prolog

The events described in this collection of short stories are true. At least as true as I was able to make them, being forced to rely on my memory, which at times had to be stretched back in time as much as sixty plus years!

These recorded adventures are but short blips in the span of time in which they were experienced, but are some of the most vivid memories that I have saved and cherish from my youth.

The people who shared these experiences with me, and allowed me to experience them in the first place, were without a doubt the main force that shaped my personality and charted the course that was set for the remainder of my life.

I fully realize that I was, and still am, very lucky to grow and continue to live in such a pristine, wonderful piece of the world. I truly wish all children could receive the same opportunities I had!

And now, the Adventures begin!

# How I Learned; "Summer is Mostly for Kids"

I suppose if everyone in the whole wide world had a say so on the subject of seasons, most of 'um would vote summer as their favorite season. I'd be in the minority. But summer would be my second choice. I'm a fall person. But most of all, summer is pretty darn good. Still...as I already said, summer is mostly for kids.

Oh don't get me wrong. Everybody can have lots of fun doing lots of summer stuff. Lots more than you can do in winter, fall or spring. But shoot, sometime springs don't even show up here in the north woods. Sometimes it jumps from winter right into summer. Dad said that up here in the north woods, spring is mostly a myth. And when I was real young, I thought "myth" was a month in the year when spring was supposed to show up.

I guess my first memories of what summer was like started when I was about three. That would make it 1940. Most of what I remember, about way back then, was Dad and Mom and Uncle Bud workin' like the devil all the daylight hours trying to make our home just a tad bit nicer by adding a porch to the Old Homestead.

But maybe I'd better tell you how we got to he north wood in the first place. Otherwise, summers, as well as the other three seasons, would have been a whole lot different for my family and me.

Without the Great Depression, I'd probably growed up to be a farmer. Nothin' wrong with that! The whole darn world'd be in a sorry mess if nobody was a farmer. I'm just sayin' my whole life got changed, (as did millions of others) by that old depression. Like most country folks back then, both sides of my family were farmers.

Mountain, Wisconsin, where I was born, isn't the greatest farming area by any stretch of the imagination. Dad Anderson called it "The great rock pile." But to many of the immigrants from northern Europe it sure looked a lot like home to them. But the climate and soil wasn't much like home, and tryin' to make a livin' by farming a rock pile was nearly an impossible job.

When the Great Depression rolled around, Dad Anderson, like thousands of others, lost the family farm. The local bank foreclosed on the property in 1932. Still being a single man, he hitchhiked north a hundred miles and discovered the north woods. And he fell in love with it!

Well, to make a long story a bit shorter, he knocked around the Minocqua, WI area until 1935 before returning to Mountain and marrying his high school sweet heart. Esther was the only daughter in the Jorgensen household, along with four brothers.

By 1938 Dad and Edward, one of the Jorgensen brother in laws, scraped up enough money to buy forty acres of pristine woods and water in the township of St. Germain in Vilas County. It cost a whole $120.00! The "40" contained over a quarter mile of shoreline on the north shore of a tiny twenty six-acre lake, then called "Dollar Lake". And best of all, not another house existed anywhere on the rest of the shore line!

During the summer of '38, Dad and two of the Jorgensen brothers hauled lumber to the lake from Mountain. They had purchased an old barn for $10.00, and the used lumber became the building material for what would be our new home. While the construction of the one room log cabin dragged on, Mom Anderson and the kid, who had arrived in February of 1937, lived with grandpa and grandma Jorgensen back in Mountain.

And in early October of 1939, Dad and Mom loaded up the '35 Chevy pickup with all our meager possessions and headed to "The Lake". A new life for all three of us loomed ahead!

The entry in Dad's diary for the date of our arrival to our new home is a gem. "Arrived at the lake today. Have $6.38 to our name and no job. Looks like a long winter ahead." That it was, along with many more! But we survived and grew stronger because of the adversity. Everybody can learn a lot, living with adversity.

By the time my tiny brain was finally big enough to start storin' stuff, it was the summer of 1940. Uncle Bud had built partitions in the one room cabin, creating two small bedrooms. A dock got built down the hill at the lake, along with an ice house. A small one stall garage, with an attached shed roof, provided a place to keep our truck out of the weather, plus a woodshed. The wilderness was slowly giving way to civilization.

Most of what I remember, other than all the work the adults did, was playin' with a few toys and our two mutt dogs, Jip and Chum, in a pile of sand we called our front yard. It was nice and quiet at the lake during that wonderful summer of 1940 and what more could a three year old kid want besides a sandbox, two pals and two parents that loved and took care of ya?

Dad finally found a job with the WPA helping build a new red brick two room school to replace the old one room wooden model that had served the children of St. Germain for many years. The crew worked ten hours a day and was paid $1.81 for their efforts. Just think, a whole $9.05 a week! But it was enough for us to exist. Then in 1941 Dad obtained a license which made him a professional fishing guide. That license cost $1.00. And the $6.00 per day fee he charged for his services really added up. At least during the summer months.

Uncle Bud, who just kinda got adopted into our family, landed a job with the Department of Conservation, and his pay check helped put a little more food on the table. We weren't getting rich, but as Dad often said about stuff like that, "It's better than a kick in the arse with a frozen boot."

The summers of '41 and '42 just kind of blend together as a dreamy kind of kid's memory. There ain't much storage space in a kid's brain when he's that young. But by the fall of '42 things changed, which would make summers a lot more memorable. I got sent off to that new school Dad had helped build!

School was o.k. In fact, I really liked school, once I got used to the idea that Mrs. Polzin was in charge. I found a life long friend named Tom Dean, learned how to read, write, cipher, and sit in one place for hours on end. But being cooped up in a two room country school with fifty to sixty other kids, made those quiet, carefree summer days at The Lake look a lot better!

But other events caused changes in my routine for the summer of '43. Dad and Uncle Bud completed yet another building overlooking The Lake. It was a tad smaller than The Homestead, and became the first of three additional building that would eventually be named "Anderson's Cottages", and later still, "Kasomo Lodge". We were in the business of housing tourists!

Oh, the tourists and their money didn't start pouring in right away! In fact, I can't really say money poured in at any time during the thirty two years our resort was in business. But that resort business sure changed summers!

My carefree days of fishin' off the dock for perch, sunfish and an occasional stray bass, catchin' frogs, playin' with Jip and Chum, and in general just doin' whatever I pleased, came to a screechin' halt. Suddenly I had chores!

Yes sir, we were a mighty proud family when Dad and Mom hung out our first sign on Highway C.

# Anderson's Cottages

## Rustic Housekeeping Cottage for Rent

The sign was in basic black and white, Like the movies and just about everything in the whole world back in the 40's. Why, with a big World War going on, about the only other color you saw was our army's olive green, and the red, white and blue American Flag or pictures of Uncle Sam. But that sign hanging on those two cedar posts, which beckoned summer tourists to our doorstep, began a great change in our lives that continues in mine till this day!

As I said earlier, the tourists and the money they brought up north with them didn't pour in, it kinda started to dribble in, and in a few years increased to a tickle. But it was money! And with it, the wolf, who according to Mom and Dad, was always lurking just outside our door, was driven a litter deeper into the surrounding forest. And for Mom and Dad, that was an especially good feeling!

Our sign indicated Anderson's Cottages were "rustic". Although by north woods standards, we considered them "modern". By city folks standards, they were probably just a little bit less than "primitive".

Two additional cabins were built, bringing the total to three, and they were always spotlessly cleaned by Mom. Our cabins, (or cottages as we preferred to call them) didn't provide any of the luxuries that city slickers were used to having. But not having any idea of how people lived outside the north woods, I had no way of knowing what "luxury" was. I figured that living in such a wonderful, beautiful, peaceful, place as the north woods, staying warm, being well fed and loved was enough. I guess I might still feel that way if I hadn't been spoiled by all the modern stuff that has come along in the last half century.

Well, to start off with, we had no electricity. We conquered darkness with kerosene lamps and Coleman gas lanterns. No electricity meant no running water. We supplied this with a handy hand pump at the kitchen sink. And there was a hand pump in each cottage. No running water meant no inside toilets. We solved this problem by building a "two holer" outhouse a few yards from each cabin. The luxury in this department was real toilet paper in the outhouses, not a Sears or Wards catalog that some resorts often substituted for the real thing.

No electricity also meant no refrigerators. But we did supply "modern" ice boxes. The blocks of ice Dad and Uncle Bud cut by hand out of The Lake during the winter were stored under mountains of sawdust in the icehouse. A thirty pound block of ice would keep your food from spoilin' for several days. And if you wanted to cool off a drink of some kind, a whack or two with the ever handy ice pick would get you a chunk of crystal clear ice that would do the trick.

If the weather got a bit chilly, you could heat up the cabin with a rip roaring wood fire in the pot bellied cast iron stove. If it got too hot, you just opened a window and let he cool northern breeze do the coolin'. Or, you could sit on the screened in porch and watch mosquitoes try to get in out of the mid day heat.

When it was time to cook a meal, the propane gas three burner hot plate would heat something up in a jiffy. Telephone? Not on your life! Why'd ya want to be bothered by a ringin' phone when you're on vacation? Besides, the phone lines were over three miles away from our property. So anyway, the chores began and some of my carefree time evaporated.

Looking back, (it's been over a half century of time, and that's a long way to look back) the chores weren't so bad after all. But to a kid in his subteen years, most anything labeled a "Chore" or "Work", is viewed in a different light. Usually a shade of black.

Filling the ice boxes was the worst! First you had to dig down through the wet sawdust to a layer of ice. Then you had to pry loose one of those hundred pound plus blocks of lake ice. Then you rolled it out of the icehouse and watched it land "ker-plunk" in the sand. After replacing the sawdust, an ice saw was used to cut two deep groves in the top of the ice. One groove was north and south, the other east and west, creating a cross which divided the block roughly in quarters. Then with a ice spud, (that a tool like a spear, except square on the tip instead of pointed) you would pound it into the groves until the ice block split into four pieces. Now the easy part was over.

Next, each piece was loaded into the wheelbarrow and taken to The Lake to be washed free of sawdust. Then it was up the hill to cottage number one and repack the ice compartment in the ice box so it'd be plumb full. Under each ice box was a dishpan which collected the water from the melting ice. It had to be emptied each time the ice box was filled. Next the sequence was repeated for cabins two and three, plus The Homestead.

The daily chores continued, although not necessarily in this order. The wood boxes were checked, and filled if necessary. Each cottage needed to have the fuel in the lamps and lanterns checked, and filled. Then the outhouses needed sweeping, the boats were cleaned, beach area policed for litter. Raking up the continuous falling pine needles and hauling them into the woods was no delight either. Another wonderful experience was collecting the garbage and storing it in the fifty five gallon barrels by the fish cleaning house. If someone had cleaned fish, I needed to carry the innards out in the woods and bury them deep enough so Jip and Chum or some other hungry critter like coyotes, wolves, foxes or bears, skunks or raccoons wouldn't dig them up. Although something usually did.

After all that, I checked in with Mom. Dad called her "The Admiral", 'cause she was in charge of runnin' the resort. Mom was never hard to find. She was either in the kitchen cookin', cleanin', or cannin' something. If not there she'd be in the laundry washin' sheets, pillow cases, towels or just plain clothes. With the tourists came lots more washin'. If it was nice out she'd be hangin' stuff on the clotheslines to dry or takin' stuff down if it was dry. And then came the foldin' and pilin', and...boy did that woman work! (And even now at 88 she still hasn't slowed down much!) If Mom had no additional official directives, I was free to be a carefree kid. At least till tomorrow and the dreaded chores again.

Actually, there was two kinds of carefree. First there was the kind of carefree when tourists brought kids along who were about my age. Then I had someone to play with, besides Jip and Chum. We could fish, swim, explore or do whatever our little hearts desired. Of course, during my pre-teen years girls didn't count. (Boy oh boy did that rule change later!)

The second kind of carefree was when just old people, over the age of fifteen, were staying in our cottages. Then Jip, Chum and I had to find our own fun. Just the three of us. But finding fun things to do never seemed to be a problem.

During the summer months we had neighbors. That's if you count someone living a half mile away as being a neighbor. These folks had a summer cottage south of us on what was then Highway C, where they spent most of the summer. There were two boys in the family, both older than me, but not by much. The older brother was kinda bossy most of the time, so we never hit it off too good. The younger brother was only a year older than me and we soon became good pals. But there was a slight problem with communication. My new pal was deaf, and couldn't speak or hear.

Grandma Jorgensen, who spent the summers with us helping Mom with all the work, said my new pal was "deef and dumb". I knew he was deaf, but never figured out why Grandma thought he was dumb. In fact, he was real smart. My new pal lost no time in teaching me sign language so we could talk to each other! Now if that ain't bein' smart, I don't know what is.

Well anyway, I really did have lots of time to be carefree one way or another. I guess being an only child gave me lots of practice in learnin' how to take care of myself. And as I got older, I discovered that's a real good piece of education.

One thing I did miss more and more as summer rolled around, was Dad. His guiding career had really taken off and generally he spent ninety to over a hundred days out on the lakes helping the tourists catch some fish. Findin' and catchin' fish just came naturally to him. And his friendly, outgoing personality attracted customers like a magnet.

Of course I understood why Dad guided so much. We needed the money. And guide's wages were inching up. By the time I pinned on my first guide badge in 1953, the daily rate had zoomed to $15.00. Although Dad considered me an apprentice and I only collected $7.50 a day.

But even though Dad and I didn't get to do much stuff together in the summer, he really make up for it in the fall and winter. All in all I was a dang lucky kid. But it would take a few more summer before I realized just how lucky I was.

Another person who helped fill in some of my carefree time was Grandma Jorgensen. She was the only grandparent I really got to know. And she was a sweetheart! Both of my Anderson grandparents died before I was born, so all I ever knew about them were stories from Dad and my Anderson Uncles. Grandpa Jorgenson died when I was about two years old, so I only was able to store a couple of brief, fleeting memories of Grandpa Chris.

One of Grandma Jorgensen's favorite pastimes was pickin' berries. And boy could she pick! She'd bring me along mainly just to carry the full buckets home, even though she tried her best to make a picker out of me. She wasted lots of time on that project.

Grandma's knurled fingers could snatch berries off those bushes quicker than a brook trout could suck up a bug. On the other hand, sending me into a berry patch was like letting a tornado loose in a glass factory. I dropped three out of four berries I picked, usually knocked most of the others off the vines, and wound up eating the one I picked. As you can guess, my bucket rarely had it's bottom covered. Grandma must have said a hundred times, "My stars child, you sure are clumsy!" And who could argue the point?

Grandma and I usually started pickin' wild strawberries in late June. Then by early to mid July the blueberries were ripe. That is if the frost we usually got in May hadn't killed all the blossoms. By mid to late July the raspberries were ready for harvest and by mid to late August we cleaned up on blackberries. Sometimes the whole family would team up for a cranberry harvest in last September.

Most of those berries got canned and did a nice job of helping to fill the shelves that lined the walls of our root cellar under The Homestead. All winter long Mom would make jams and jellies and other yummy stuff, which still makes my mouth water just thinking about it. But in reality, it was lots of work. Although nobody punched a time clock.

I lost my two buddies, Jip and Chum, when I was about six or seven. Chum was quite the bum and often was absent from our home for several days. He just ran off one day and never came back. Dad and Uncle Bud figured a wolf probably got him. We had lots of timber wolves roaming the country back then, so that's probably what happened.

Jip had a nasty habit of chasing deer. We never could break him of it, and one day while Uncle Ed was hunting he caught him in the act. So he shot him. Jip I mean. At the time I was awfully upset, but if you ever get to see what dogs do to a fawn after they hamstring it, you'd understand why dogs that chase deer need to be stopped. One way or another.

Dad replaced Jip and Chum with a black cocker spaniel. We named him Pat. And he was a real dog! Great hunter and smart as a whip! But we only had him a couple of years. One day while Grandma and I were pickin' berries next to the highway, Pat chased a chipmunk across the road and a car hit him. He died in my arms. I never cried so hard in my life. But Dad went right out and got another black cocker and named him Pat. He became my best friend and gave me a lifetime of great memories. Old Pat died during my first year in college. I cried then too.

As the years passed, as they do all too quickly, the range of my activities broadened. I discovered girls had better uses than pushing them off the dock, or tossing them off the diving raft, or putting mud in their hair, or slipping a wet frog into their bathing suit, or some other disgusting display of juvenile male stupidity.

I discovered the game of softball was awfully fun to play, and got fairly good at it too. I joined a men's fast pitch league when I was fifteen. And I played as a regular. I even got good enough to be selected to the local All-Star Teams in '53 and '54. Our reward was being able to play games against "The King and His Court" a four man softball tem that continues to tour the world playing and defeating teams using nine men. I continued to play organized summer softball for the next forty years. I might still be out there pitching and hitting if my right knee hadn't forced my retirement.

Dad bought a sawmill just before World War II ended, and I saved the culled boards and some of the better slabs to build the "Mother of all Tree Houses". It was a two story job and provided hundred of hours of fun until the "Mother of all Wind Storms" scattered it's remains over several acres.

As the summers slipped away, lots of changes occurred on the Anderson Property, as well as to our lives. Dad and Mom bought an additional eighty acres for $3.00 an acre, from which Dad harvested pine and spruce logs to saw up and build The Lodge, a laundry building, and a new ice house.

Electricity finally arrived in November of 1946, the day before deer season. We finally got on an eight party, "party line" phone line in 1950.

With the coming of electric power, out went the ice boxes, the kerosene lamps, and the hand pumps. In came electric lights, hot and cold running water, with showers, and propane gas heaters. Luxury finally arrived at Anderson's Cottages.

The Conservation Department changed the name of "The Lake" from "Dollar Lake" to "Kasomo Lake". Local lore has it that three couples once camped on it's shores back in the '20's. One version even suggested the visitors had built a crude log cabin. The story states that one couple was from Kansas, one from South Dakota and the third was from Missouri. Hence, "Ka-So-Mo". Dad always told our guests that "Kasomo" was Indian word that meant "Lake of many fish". Well, it did have lots of fish.

With the advent of running water, the old ice house by the lake was torn down and a new one was built next to the fish cleaning house. Even though we no longer used the ice boxes, we kept our guest's fish refrigerated in the ice house. When our guests got ready to head back to the city, we'd pack their fish in a box with ice, sawdust and sphagnum moss. The moss retained the moisture and kept the packed fish fresh for days. The moss was harvested from a nearby swamp. That was another chore on my list.

Mom got tired of cooking meals for our visiting tourists after the summer of 1959. We returned to just being a "housekeeping resort". Dad passed away in 1961, just 52 years of age. That was a tragedy I never quite got over. Mom ran the resort with the help of my wife, Peggy, and I until 1966 and then sold it to us. We continued the "Anderson Tradition" through the tourist season of 1975 and sold the resort and it's lake frontage to developers in the spring of '76. An era had ended.

Peggy and I built a new home on one of the "back 40's", where I now sit and record this trivial bit of history. Our four kids and their families live fairly close by and our four grandchildren visit often. Some of what I did during my youthful, carefree days is still being done.

I guess when all is said and done, I probably did just about everything a boy growing up in the north woods can do. At least one who is allowed to try. Not all kids get that chance, to try I mean. And that is another tragedy!

But summers only last a few months, often less in the unpredictable north country. And those carefree days of summer become those carefree days of fall, winter, and spring. That is if you're a kid. Or a grown up who still knows how to think like a kid!

# Campin' Is Lots Of Fun, Until It Gets Dark

I guess when you're a young kid, there are lots of stuff that gets you excited, even if you don't know nothin' about it. And young kids seldom do. Know much about anything I mean.

Well, that's how I got into goin' on my first campin' trip. Gettin' excited and not knowin' nothin' about campin'. But my cousin, Lee, was an expert on the subject. At least he though he was.

It was the summer of 1946. I was nine years old and cousin Lee was much more mature at eleven. And, Cousin Lee had bought a tent! It was one of those army surplus jobs that was supposed to sleep two men. It would have too, if both men happened to be midgets.

The tent was a drab olive green color, like everything the army made for World War II. It was about six feet long and three feet wide and stood about three and a half feet tall at the peak. Just the right size for a couple of skinny kids. But it smelled like mill dewed rubber. That's because it was made of rubber and had got all mill dewed being stored in some old army warehouse. But Cousin Lee said the smell would go away after we had the tent set up out in the fresh air for a few hours. I believed him, 'cause he was older than me and knew lots about tents and campin'. Little de we know we'd both learn a few more things about campin', and in short order!

It was the first week in July. Cousin Lee's dad and mom, Uncle Shuck and Aunt Minda as they were known, hauled Cousin Lee and all his campin' gear up to The Lake in St. Germain from their home in Rhinelander, Wisconsin. After visiting my Dad and Mom for a couple of hours, Uncle Shuck and Aunt Minda wished the two young campers "Good Luck" and headed back home to Rhinelander. Me and Cousin Lee had already started "the list".

I found out right off from Cousin Lee that before anyone could go campin' they had to make out a list. On their list campers write down everything they need to survive in the wilderness for however long the camping trip was supposed to last. Cousin Lee even suggested we add a few things to the list that we didn't expect to need, cause who knows what a couple of campers might need unexpectedly. Cousin Lee dictated the list of stuff and I printed it on the back of an old grocery sack from the A & P store.

"O.K. Buckshot", Cousin Lee dictated, "One tent, two sleeping bags, two pillows, our fishin' poles, two dozen candy bars, a bag of popcorn, all the comic books we can find, a case of soda pop, one frying pan, one dozen eggs, two pounds of bacon, flour, salt and pepper, two loaves of bread, one ax, two knives, hammer and nails, rope, matches, dry firewood, extra socks and clean underwear, extra pants, two pairs of hip boots, four dozen worms, two flashlights, candles, and let's see, did I forget anything? Oh ya, two caps."

I had two questions. "Where we gonna get all that stuff and how in heck are we gonna get it all down to the crick where we're gonna camp?" I should have known that Cousin Lee had the minor problems all worked out.

"Simple Buckshot. We'll beg some of the food from your dad and mom, I already brought some of the stuff from home. Then we'll pool all the money we've been savin' for this campin' trip and walk up to Weber's Bar and Wildlife Farm to buy whatever else we still have on the list. As to gettin' all our stuff down to our secret campin' spot on the crick, we'll haul it all down in your wagon".

I was embarrassed at how stupid I was, not being able to figure all those problems out so quick. But then again, Cousin Lee was older and therefore much smarter than I was.

Early the next morning we started gathering the stuff on our list and making preparations to start moving it to our secret campin' spot. And we had a neat place to stockpile our massive quantity of supplies.

Dad and Mom Anderson were in the process of building a brand new home for us. A hole in the ground for the basement had bee dug a year earlier and Dad, with the help of Uncle Bud Jorgensen and Uncle Art Anderson, were almost done laying the cement block walls. The walled area, being nearly complete, gave us lots of privacy and security from prying adult eyes. We sure didn't want any adults telling us how to go about getting ready for this camping adventure. After all, we had it all figured out ourselves!

Cousin Lee and I even invented a name for this blocked fortress. "Fort Apache". We had been to Randolph Scott western movie and saw a fort named Fort Apache. We figured if it was a good enough name for a western hero like Randolph Scott, it was good enough for us too!

Dad, Uncle Bud and Uncle Art were all down at the sawmill cutting up some pine logs for lumber to finish building our new home. Mom was busy baking bread, so we had Fort Apache all to ourselves.

By mid-morning we had assembled all available supplies. We were still short a few items. a check of our list indicated we still needed the case of soda pop, two dozen candy bars, a bag of popcorn and a few more comic books. A check of our financial situation resulted in a combined net worth of $12.85. Why heck, we had way more money than we would need to buy the rest of our supplies at Weber's Bar and Wildlife Farm! We had this campin' plan worked out to the last fine detail. I guess Cousin Lee really did know his stuff!

We loaded my red wagon with the tent, sleeping bags, the ax, hammer, nails and rope. We tied everything in place with rope and headed down the dusty dirt road toward our secret campin' spot. But...we had to pass the sawmill.

The mill was hummin' away, sawin' up those big pine logs, so we thought we might sneak by without being spotted. No Chance! Dad and our uncles had eyes in the backs of their heads. But to our surprise, they only gave us a brief look and went right on with the sawin'! We did detect a slightly evil smirk on their faces. But adults often look at kids like that. And you never know what they're thinkin' when they do it. That's the worst part.

Our "Secret Spot" was tucked inside an alder ticket right on the bank of Lost Crick, about a half mile from our resort. Cousin Lee and I had found this super campin' spot a little over a year ago when we were spearin' suckers during their spring spawning run. Dad always smoked a batch of sucker every spring, and Cousin Lee and I had finally been deemed old enough to do some of the spearin'. Boy, did we have fun! And we only broke one of Dad's pitch forks when I hit a big rock instead of the sucker I was aimin' at.

First we cut enough brush to allow the tent to be placed in the alder thicket. Then we set up the tent and stashed the sleeping bags inside. Boy, did that tent stink! We hammered in the tent stakes and secured the sides and ends with pieces of rope. Nobody would find us here. Not even Randolph Scott! The olive green tent blended in almost perfectly with green leaves of the alders.

It took three more trips with my wagon to haul all the remaining supplies to the camp site. A fourth trip was made to the sawmill to get a load of nice dry slab wood for our fire. The three workers gave us a couple of sly grins, but just kept on a sawin'.

Next we chopped down two small maple trees and made a crude foot bridge from our campsite to a tiny sand island in the middle of the crick. It was here we'd build our fire to make sure we didn't set the woods ablaze. As I told you before, we had all the angles figured out!

It was mid afternoon when we finished our bridge. We still needed to make a trip to Weber's Bar and Wildlife Farm to buy the rest of our supplies. And Weber's was nearly a mile away. The old dirt road, named "Deadman's Gulch", ran from our resort past the crick where we were camped, and out to Highway C where Weber's Bar was located. Taking turns pulling the empty wagon, we arrived at our destination in less than a half hour. Mr. Weber was more than happy to help us secure our supplies. And just before we left his store, we spied something that wasn't on our list. And we just had to buy some!

3

As I mentioned earlier, it was the first week of July. In fact, the date was July 3rd. And what do kids like to do on the 4th of July? Well, everyone know you got to shoot off some firecrackers on the 4th of July! And Mr. Weber had all kinds of firecrackers! With the remained of our money we bought as many as we could. And that was nearly a hundred! Boy would we have fun tomorrow, blasting off those 'crackers down by the crick. And best of all, our parent would never know!

Supper consisted of a half dozen little rock bass we caught out of the deep hole just below the old wooden logging dam, which was only a few yards downstream from our camp. We fried up a little bacon and then burned the fish in the hot grease. That, with a couple of slices of Mom's homemade bread, made the main course. A couple of soda pops and a candy bar or two filled us up real good. Why, we could probably live out here off the land forever,...if we wanted to.

We were in our tent reading some comics books, with dusk just settling in, when we heard the sound of a car engine. We looked at each other and silently wondered, "Who could be drivin' down that old dirt road at this time of the day?" Then we heard two car doors slam shut. We crawled out of our tent to investigate.

You know, it's downright amazin' sometimes how lucky grownups can be. Imagine, Dad and Mom stopped their truck on that old dirt road not fifty feet from where we had hid our tent! And as soon as they stepped out of that truck,...why, they spotted us! I suppose if we'd put out our fire they wouldn't have seen the smoke. But then again,...they might have spied on us earlier and knew just where we were camped. Ya, that musta been it. They spied on us earlier. "Cause where we had pitched our tent, even Randolph Scott couldn't have found us!

Dad and Mom were real impressed with our campin' area. Dad said we'd done a right nice job of settin' everything up. He was real happy to see our fire had been built on the sand island. That was "usin' your head", as he put it. But what Dad and Mom didn't think was such a good idea was the sack of firecrackers they spotted just inside our tent. We had some explainin' to do!

Mom voted to confiscate the whole bag. Dad thought it over for a few seconds and voted to let us keep them! A tie! After a brief discussion, Mom reluctantly gave in. I couldn't believe it! Usually a breach of conduct like buying firecrackers without permission earned at least a week of being "grounded". Or worse! Wow! Were we lucky! Cousin Lee and I thanked Mom and Dad for letting us keep our treasures and promised to be careful and not blow any of our fingers off. Dad smiled and told us that sounded like a good idea. Mom still looked unsure their decision was sound.

After a few more minutes of lookin' around, Dad and Mom said they'd better be gettin' back home, as it was GETTING DARK, and they were sure we'd want to crawl into our sleeping bags and get a good nights sleep. Then they walked to their truck.

Cousin Lee and I were besides ourselves with joy! We had gotten out of what usually would have been a nasty mess. And now we could get back to the business of enjoyin' our campin' trip. Then Dad added one final suggestion.

"Hey!", Dad yelled at us from the running board of his truck, "I just thought of a good use for those firecrackers." We waited for his suggestion. "When you hear a BEAR sniffin' around your tent, just light a firecracker and toss it outside. That'll scare him off in nothin' flat. Good night. Sleep tight!" And off they drove.

Cousin Lee and I looked at each other with horror written all over our faces! BEARS!!!!! BEARS!!!!!! Oh my God! There are bears in these woods! Big, black, mean, kid eatin' bears! Why, they' rip through this old flimsy army tent with one swipe of their claw infested paw! We'd better be on guard!

As the sound of the truck's motor died in the distance, we turned on our flashlights and pretended to read comic books. But now, as our minds began to fill with growing horror, we noticed the surrounding forest was beginning to emit strange sounds. Sounds that even Cousin Lee couldn't identify.

There were "chirps", and "squeaks", and "hums", and "croaks", and "whines", and "buzzing". And then... the most terrifying sound known to man,...a twig snapped!

Two matches blazed into brightness, followed by the hissing sound of burning fuses. Two sparkling projectiles were tossed into the blackness beyond the door of our tent. "CRACK!" "KAPOW!" The night was ripped by the exploding sounds of two Black Cat firecrackers. All the chirps, squeaks, hums, croaks, whines, and buzzing stopped! There, that took care of that problem. Nothing would come within a mile of this camp now! We went back to reading our comic books.

But within minutes the sounds were back again, including the snapping twig. And this time it seemed closer! "POW!" "KABOOM!", two more sound ending explosions rocked the night. Once again the savage noises were silenced. But not for long!

As the night blackened more and more, the range and volume of the noises being generated by the demons of the night increased. The time between explosions narrowed. By eleven o'clock our supply of firecrackers had been exhausted. The beams cast by our flashlights grew dimmer and dimmer. Sheer panic set in!

I don't remember who screamed it first, but one of us, or perhaps both of us in unison suggested, "LET'S GET OUR OF HERE!!!!"

While it had taken us nearly a half hour to put our tent up, it was down and crammed into my wagon in about twelve seconds. Our sleeping bags, and whatever we could pile on top of the load was quickly secured with rope. What we couldn't carry or pack was simply left where it lay. The wheels of my wagon probably only touched the ground two or three times all the way home.

The hundred yard stretch of road through the "Minnow Pond Swamp" was pure terror beyond belief! Our feeble flashlight beams couldn't begin to penetrate the dense fog that engulfed the narrow road and swirled around our bodies. Wild, hungry beasts of unknown origins lurked just beyond our vision. We raced onward, not caring what might fall from our wagon. We had to get home! Surely, packs of snarling, blood thirsty creatures were probably gaining on us! We ran as though the very Devil himself was nipping at our heels!

Once clear of the fog shrouded swamp, the road rose sharply upward. Still we ran on, huffing and puffing like steam locomotives. Our hearts were pounding in our throats as though they would burst. Home was still a quarter of a mile distance.

Our pace began to slow, as our legs started to feel like melting butter. Suddenly, a huge black shape loomed in our path! The hairs on the back of our necks stood straight out. Expecting to be violently attacked by this yet unknown monster, we skidded to a halt. But then I recognized the "monster". It was the skid-way full of pine logs at Dad's sawmill! We were nearly home to safety! Security was only another hundred yards away! We ran on with renewed energy!

It was probably about midnight when we stumbled through the door way of our newly constructed basement, Fort Apache. We slammed the door shut and threw the bolt closed. And collapsed on the sandy basement floor.

Cousin Lee and I lay in the sand for several minutes to allow our breathing to return somewhat to normal and allow our hearts to work themselves from our throats back to our chests. What a great feeling it was to have escaped certain death! But now we were safe. The high cement walls of Fort Apache would keep us protected from any and all monsters, bears or other demons. We could once again pitch our tent and sleep in the sincere knowledge that no harm would befall us. We slept soundly until morning.

Uncle Art was an early riser. He awakened shortly after sunrise, quietly dressed, and slipped out of my parent's house. He decided to walk down to the creek and see how the two young campers had survived their first night in the wilderness.

Within a half hour Uncle Art had returned to our home, with a mystery on his hands. Mom, Dad and Uncle Bud had awakened and were wondering where Uncle Art had gone. As he burst through the kitchen door the worried look on his face brought the trio of onlookers to attention.

"The kids have disappeared!", he began. "I took a walk down to the old dam where you said they were camping, and they're gone! Tent and all!".

Mom nearly fainted. "Oh my God!" she exclaimed, "I knew something would happen to them if we were foolish enough to let them go camping at their age. We've got to find them!"

Dad scratched his chin and grinned a little grin. "I know them kids. They moved their camp after we horned in on 'um last evening. I bet they didn't move their camp very far. Art and I'll drive down with the truck and find 'um. Don't fret."

As Dad and Uncle Art started for the truck, something coming from the inside of our yet to be completed basement caught their eye. A thin column of blue smoke was slowly twisting skyward into a bright, sunny, morning sky. Dad slowly climbed one of the ladders that was leaning on the outside of Fort Apache's walls. He peered over the highest cement blocks. What he saw brought out one of his finest belly laughs.

Gathered around a campfire were the two missing campers. Breakfast was in the making as some bacon and eggs sizzled in a blackened cast iron frying pan. Two heads spun around as one at the sound of Dad's laughter. And two faces definitely reflected a blush of embarrassment.

Well, "the story" had to be told. We glossed over the part abut running pell mell for our lives, but I seem to suspect the adults knew we fled in panic without us 'fessing up to the fact.

Cousin Lee stayed around for another week or so and camp we did! That first experience had taught us a valuable lesson about campin'! And the remainder of our campin' went off without a hitch.

Fort Apache sure was a nice place to camp!

# Every Lake Needs Some Clams

When I was just a kid, I got real excited about a lot of stuff. (Come to think of it, a half century later I still do!) But back when I was a kid and Memorial Day week end rolled around, I got a special kind of excited. I'd get to knock around with two of my best buddies for nearly a week! Maybe that don't sound like somethin' that would create a special kind of excited to some folks, but I only got to see these special buddies a couple of times a year, and then only for a few days. Ya see, they lived a whole long ways away from where I lived. They lived in a big city called Chicago.

I first met Johnny and Eddie when I was eight. They were brothers. Johnny was a year older than me and Eddie a year younger. Their dad hired my dad to do some guiding and catch him some fish. Mom was working at the same resort where Johnny, Eddie and his folks were stayin', tryin' to increase the dribble of money into our pockets. So I got dragged along every day to be carefree around the resort while Mom baked cakes, pies and other assorted yummy stuff which was served to the tourists who stayed there. Dad did most of his guiding out of the same resort, so for several summers the entire Anderson family spent much of their time at Clear View Lodge on Big St. Germain Lake. For me, it was like bein' on a three month vacation for free.

Clear View Lodge was really big compared to our little resort, which at the time had but one cabin to rent. Clear View had fifteen! So there was always a few kids my age to be carefree with. And me bein' a "native", why I taught them lots of stuff about the north woods. Whether they wanted to be taught or not! Well anyway, Johnny, Eddie and me hit it off real good and over the years I got them into more north woods stuff than you can shake a stick at. And boy did we have fun!

"The Great Clam Transplant" took place during the early summer of 1948. By then the three of us had all matured to the extent that our folks kinda kicked us out of their hair in the morning and really didn't care to see us until dark. That is, after my chores got done. And with two helpers, it didn't take long to get the chores all finished. After that, it was off on one great adventure after another. "The Great Clam Transplant" was one of our most memorable.

My memory is somewhat hazy as how exactly we decided to go clam hunting, but seems to me it had something to do with all the mud in "The Lake". On this particular day in history, the three of us were fishin' for perch in the little lake where I lived. We were using one of the boats owned by "Anderson's Cottages". Somehow, during a lull in the catchin', our conversation drifted into questioning why The Lake had so much mud in it,

8

while Big St. Germain for instance, had almost none. After sorting out all the possible scientific facts about the two bodies of water, we deduced the answer to our question was "clams".

Now you might be wonderin' about the connection between "mud" and "clams". Well, we knew that clams crawled around on the bottoms of lakes and cricks, with their big slimy tongues sticking in the sand. And all the lakes and cricks I knew of that had clams in them were fairly clear and free of mud. So, it didn't take a rocket scientist to figure out that clams must eat up all the mud and keep the lake or crick clean. I guess you'd call that "scientific deduction".

Seeing as The Lake didn't have any clams living in it, we were sure that was the reason it contained so much mud. So, to clean up all that yukky mud, all we had to do was gather some clams and transplant them into The Lake! And then for sure, in a few years all that mud would be gone and we'd have a nice sandy bottomed lake! And I knew where we could collect all the clams we wanted in no time at all! It just goes to show you how concerned we were about the environment, even way back in the 40's.

It took but a few minutes to return to the dock and begin to gather all the equipment we'd need to harvest some clams. First, we'd need Mom's biggest washtub to hold all the clams while we transported them from their old home in Lost Crick to their new home in The Lake. Next, we put Mom's washtub in Dad's wheelbarrow, which would be the vehicle to do the haulin'. Third, we needed a pitch fork to pry those big old clams out of the sand and gravel they lived in on the bottom of the crick. And last but not least, we needed hip boots and waders to keep us dry while we did the harvestin'. And seein' that Dad and Uncle Bud weren't home, we'd just borrow their boots and waders. Within a half hour we were at the crick and ready to begin our careers as environmentalists!

We left the wheelbarrow and tub on the old dirt road that ran next to the crick where we expected to end our harvest. Then we walked about a quarter of a mile further up the road and prepared to begin the clam hunt. By wading downstream it'd make our work easier, not havin' to fight the current. Johnny and I each put on a pair of oversized hip boots and we stuck Eddie into a pair of Dad's oversized waders. With those baggy waders on, Eddie kinda looked like the Pillsbury Doughboy. Eddie, bein' the youngest, usually got stuck with somethin' neither Johnny nor I wanted any part of. And a hot pair of baggy waders was one of those somethin's. Besides, Johnny and I had a special plan for Eddie and those baggy waders!

Now you might be wonderin' how we were gonna get all those ugly clams downstream to our waiting wheelbarrow and tub. Well, that's where Eddie and the baggy waders came in. As Johnny or I would pry a clam out of the crick bottom, Eddie would hold the top of the baggy waders open and

9

we' toss in the clam. Wading along downstream in the water would help make the load lighter, and by the time we got ready to exit the crick, we'd have all the clams in one place ready to dump in the washtub. When you've got scientific minds like we had, solvin' those complicated problems was easy!

By the time we reached our exit point, Eddie's waders were bulging with clams. Now he looked like the Goodyear Blimp. It was here we discovered our scientific minds had not calculated all the potential problems connected with harvesting clams and storing them in hot waders. And there were several problems!

First off, when Eddie tried to wade ashore out of the waist deep water, the load of clams in his waders became so heavy that he couldn't walk! Secondly, the clams had become mashed around Eddie's legs so tightly, that when Johnny and I dragged him to dry land, we couldn't pull him out of the waders! Thirdly, the clams, not being happy cooped up in a pair of hot waders, had, ah how should I say it, released all their internal fluids into Eddie's waders and soaked his pants!

We restarted our scientific minds to ponder our dilemma. Eddie couldn't stand up, and even if he could have gotten to his feet, he still wouldn't be able to walk. He was even beginning to complain about his legs and feet hurting. And, he also did mention something about an unpleasant odor rising from the depths of the waders.

First Johnny and I tried tipping Eddie upside down to dump out the clams. We couldn't budge him. So, we reached into the waders and pulled out the clams one by one. It was during this process that Johnny and I agreed with Eddie that there was indeed some sort of foul smelling odor in the air. And it seemed to be coming from inside his waders. But we weren't sure it came from the clams. Scientists don't jump to conclusions.

Once we had liberated the clams from the hot waders, we slid Eddie out. There was sort of a "SSSSSLLLLUUUURRRRPPPPP" sound as his legs were pulled free from the feet of the waders. Once evacuated from his prison Eddie got to his feet, which allowed Johnny and I our first good look at someone who had been cell mates with a batch of unhappy clams. From the waist down, Eddie's pants looked like they were covered with green flubber coated with donut glazing. And we now definitely decided the disgusting odor WAS coming from Dad's waders. And Eddie's pants!

I will assume few people have had the opportunity to smell the odor from the internal body fluids of calms that have been housed in hot waders for several hours. If you have, I know you have not forgotten the aroma. I would say a similar scent could be made by mixing skunk spray with some fish that have baked in the sun for several days.

We soaked Eddie and his pants in Lost Crick for about a half hour and also sloshed fresh water in and out of Dad's good waders. I had a suspicion I'd be in a lot of hot water if we didn't get the smell out.

One good thing about environmentalists, they don't give up on a project just because of a couple minor setbacks. We loaded the clams into Mom's washtub, carried the load to the waiting wheelbarrow, and by taking turns pushed it the half mile to The Lake. Then we tried doing an imitation of Bob Feller, pitching clams as far out into The Lake as we could. Thinking back on it, the clams probably weren't too happy when they settled to the bottom and discovered they were now living in a foot or more of black muck!

Later, we washed Dad's waders out with soap and warm water. After they had dried for several days, most of the smell was gone. The lucky part for me was that Dad didn't need to use his wader during the curing period. I did wait a couple of months before I told him what had happened. Dads don't usually get mad about somethin' that happened months ago. And my Dad didn't. Get mad I mean. In fact, he laughed!

Well, as the years slipped by, the amount of mud in The Lake did not diminish one bit. I guess we didn't toss in enough clams. But I never found out for sure, as I never found a clam in The Lake so I could ask one.

POSTSCRIPT: As I record this epic adventure, that we experienced in 1948, I am happy to report that both Johnny and Eddie are still counted as two of my best buddies. I don't get to see Johnny very often, but Eddie and I still manage to continue sharing adventures together!

# You Can't Mix Chubs And Trout

Back in the summer of '48 I missed my chance to become rich. Not the kind of John D. Rockefeller Sr. or Donald Trump or Michael Jordan wealthy, but rich for an eleven year old kid back in 1948. And it was all the fault of a trout.

It was a hot summer. The blazin' hot kind of summer that starts right off in May. The kind of summer that gets goin' right after winter finally gives up. The kind of summer when spring never gets a chance to wedge itself in between winter and summer. The kind of summer kids love.

Dad Anderson was booked up real solid with fishermen too. He was startin' his eighth year of pulling on the oars, guidin' those city tourists that came flockin' to the north woods once that terrible world war ended. Most folks hadn't had any vacations or time for fishin'd during the war years, and now the resorts were doin' a land office business. So were the guides.

But there was a problem durin' that hot summer of '48. The hot weather, and low water in the cricks, made it tough on the minnow dealers to get enough good bait. I guess it was a prime case of the demand outstripping the supply. (I learned about that kind of stuff a lot later in life.) So, the guides were tearin' out their hair tryin' to figure out how to get enough decent bait to keep those city fellers catchin' fish. This is where I came in.

It was early June. School had let out for the summer a couple of weeks earlier and I was happier than a hound dog in a sausage factory. My daily chores were getting a little easier to complete in less time, now that I was a maturing eleven year old, and I was having lots more time to be carefree. Dad decided to shave a little more of that carefree time off my hands and made me an offer I couldn't refuse.

"Buckshot,", he began in that low easy going tone of voice, which meant he wanted me to do something, "how'd ya like to earn a lot of money?" I hesitated slightly in answering, as I never knew anyone real close who made a lot of money.

"I guess so.", I questioningly answered. "What'd I gotta do?"

"All you have to do is fish.", Dad answered with that friendly grin of his.

Well, I'd been fishing since I was knee high to a toadstool and never got paid to do it. And I was a long ways from bein' old enough to start guiding, like Dad, so at first I thought Dad had flipped his lid. I just stared at him, not knowin' how to answer or what to ask.

12

"Well", Dad explained, "to be honest, it ain't really the kind of fishing you're used to doing." There was an awkward pause. "I want you to catch chubs."

"Catch chubs?" My face twisted into a puzzled question mark. "Catchin' chubs wouldn't be no fun. Besides, what we gonna do with chubs? They ain't big enough to eat!"

"I need good, fresh chubs to keep on guiding every day. Old Joe is having one heck of a time trying to fill his minnow tanks down at his bait stand, and with this hot weather, minnows are in short supply. Joe's got some shiners and slippery jacks, but they ain't the best bait. I need black chubs."

Well, I already knew black chubs were the toughest minnows on the planet, or at least Dad had told me more than once that they were. "So", he continued, "I'd like you to catch chubs for me and I'll pay you a nickel apiece."

Now I wasn't the best math student in fifth grade, but it didn't take me but a split second to do a five times twelve and come up with sixty. "WOW!" I yelled, "that's sixty cents a dozen! I bet I can catch eight or ten dozen a day usein' your minnow traps! Wow, am I gonna make money!"

"You can't use my minnow traps.", answered Dad.

"Why not? We use them every spring down in Lost Crick, and catch lots of chubs.", I responded.

Dad took on his serious look and explained. "Well Buckshot, there's two reasons. One, the water in Lost Crick is too warm already from all this hot weather, and the chubs have left the shallow area where we usually trap. Now they're in the deeper, cooler water way upstream where it's difficult to trap. All that's in the crick now, where we usually trap, are shiners. And they're lousy bait. All you have to do is show them a hook and they croak. (I already knew that too.)

Two, you'll have to catch chubs for me in Plum Crick. That's a cold water crick and it'll be packed to the gills with black chubs. And, as you know, Plum Crick is a trout stream and it's against the law to set minnow traps in a trout stream."

"So, how'm I supposed to catch 'um?", I inquired.

"With a hook and line, one at a time." Dad was grinning again.

Well, now I was sure Dad had flipped out into the twilight zone! Why, I had tagged along with him on a number of trout fishing expeditions to Plum Crick and we never caught any chubs. At least I never had. But then again, I had to do my fishin' from the bank, and the banks of Plum Crick were so infested with alders, balsam, spruce and cedars that it was nearly impossible to get a gob of worms in the water, say nothin' about catchin' any trout or chubs.

Dad, of course, fished in the stream with a pair of hip boots on so he could sneak up on those deep holes and yank out some of those fat, pink meat, brook trout in nothin' flat! He let me try wadin' with him a couple of times but I made so much noise splashin' and fallin' down that he said I scared every trout from Brooker's Bridge all the way down to Highway C. Dad said I was about as handy in the wadin' department as a drunken sailor on shore leave.

"With a hook and line? Ya can't catch chubs with a hook and line. The hooks too big and their mouth is too small!" For once I thought Dad didn't know what he was talkin' about. I should have knowed better.

"Yes you can. I got some size 12 hooks that I use when I tie my trout flies. I'll rig up your pole for chub catchin' and we'll take a crack at teaching you how to catch chubs right after I get back from guiding tomorrow afternoon."

And so it was! By late afternoon the following day I was standing next to Dad shiverin', as the icy waters of Plum Crick gurgled around my skinny, Levis covered legs. Dad, of course, had on his rubber hip boots. My lesson began.

O.K., now watch what I'm doin'. Chubs are always lookin' for a meal. They're a little bit like rock bass in that department. Always hungry. Notice we're out of the main flow of water, in this little backwater eddy, where their ain't much current. When we waded in, we spooked all the chubs, but if we stand real still and don't move a muscle, they'll be back in a couple of minutes. Take a look at this chub catchin' rig I fixed up on your cane pole.

My cane pole was a eight footer. Dad had tied about six feet of fine silk line to the tip and added about a foot and a half of leader material, called cat gut. And it was cat gut. That's what they made leader material out of in those days. On the end of the gut leader was the smallest hook I had ever seen, and about six inches above the hook he had squeezed on a split shot about the size of a BB. Then he covered the tip of the hook with a tiny chunk of worm. It sure didn't look much like somethin' that'd catch a fish of any kind. I wasn't impressed.

We stood in the ice cold water for another couple of minutes or so, and sure enough! A whole school of black chubs came creepin' along the bottom of the crick, and soon were swimin' all around our feet!. Dad eased the baited hook into the water and, WHAM, a feisty three inch long black chub nailed the worm covered hook! Dad yanked him out of the water, caught him in his left hand and had the hook out of tiny mouth in a split second. Then, kerplunk, the chub was dropped into the minnow bucket Dad had tied to his belt.

"There", he grinned, "now it's your turn."

I missed the first couple of "WHAMS", 'cause I didn't pull up quick enough. But on my third try I caught one. And then another, and another, and another. IT WAS EASY! I always found it hard to believe that grown ups were right so often!

Early next morning Dad rolled me out of bed and Mom filled my belly full of fried salt pork, fresh, hot Johnny Cake, and a bowl of corn meal mush. I washed it all down with a couple of glasses of milk and was ready for my first great adventure alone on Plum Crick!

As Dad and I drove down the dusty dirt road we called "Plum Creek Avenue", my worst fear surfaced. Spending five to six hours wadin' in that freezin' trout stream! But Dad had a surprise for me that I hadn't expected. I got to wear his hip boots!

Dad stuffed a couple wads of crinkled up newspaper in the toe of each boot so my size six kid feet would fit a tad better in his size nine man boots. Then he had me slip on two pairs of heavy wool socks, which would help fill in some of the vacant space, plus keep my feet toasty warm. Boy, did I feel growed up!

My adventure would begin where Brooker's Bridge crossed the crick. The early morning air was saturated with mingled scents of wildflowers, cedar and balsam. Dang that's a nice smell! The crystal clear water was making a soft gurgling sound as it slipped quickly southeast towards it's destination at Big St. Germain Lake. Dad helped me get on his hip boots, tied the baggy tops to my belt, and walked me down to the edge of the bank just below the bridge. I started to have doubts about this money makin' venture.

Then I got my final instructions. "O.K. Buckshot, now remember what I told you on the way over here. Take your time. Fish slow and easy in all the slack water eddies. Do just what I showed you yesterday. The minnow bucket will float along with you, and when you get about eight to ten dozen chubs in it, that'll be about all she'll hold.

Wade all the way down to Highway C and tie the bucket under the alders on the north side of the crick on the upstream side of the road. I'll pick up the bucket when I'm done with guidin' for the day. And watch your step. Don't trip over any logs or rocks and don't wade in water so deep that it goes over the tops of my boots and get them all soaked. You should be able to make it to the highway by noon. On your way home, stop by the mailbox and pick up the mail for your Mom. Then get your chores done. Are you ready?"

I gulped a swallow about the size of my fist and nodded my head. But my heart kept tellin' me I wasn't so sure about this whole idea. But then again, I wasn't about to chicken out now and have Dad think I was some sort of pansy. Dad gave me his best grin, patted me on my shoulder and sincerely said, "Good Luck! Start makin' some money!"

I watched Dad walk up the hill and drive off towards his destination. I looked downstream and started to think about mine. It was time to start makin' my fortune!"

The morning went just great! In a little less than four hours, Dad's minnow bucket was bulging with choice black chubs. And I even found the experience to be fun! I'd never been turned loose in quite this kind of situation before and found the solo trip down Plum Crick most interesting.

I saw a doe and her newborn fawn sneak down to the crick for a drink of water. They stood in the crick not fifteen yards from where I was quietly pounding a school of chubs. I guess I musta been real quiet, as I had never got that close to a live deer before. They sure were beautiful. Their reddish spring coats glistened in the soft morning sunlight as water dripped of their jet black noses. The little fawn kinda stumbled around in the crick and reminded me of myself, I wondered if it's mother knew anything about drunken sailors on a shore leave.

A couple of bends further, I got the wits scared out of me for a couple of seconds. A mother mallard, and about a dozen of her little fluff ball chicks, came splashing out from under the alders right next to me! Boy, stuff like that really scares the poop out of ya when ya don't expect it! Those little rascals sure could scoot!

A few minutes later a big blue heron did the same thing! He really sounded mad when he flew off, giving me several of those deep, horse voiced croaks as he headed for a new fishing location.

I also saw several muskrats, a mink, dozens of song birds, and wild flowers of all shapes and colors. I especially liked the big marsh marigolds and the beautiful long stemmed white trillium. The world was sure a beautiful place that June morning. If you took time to look around.

I was back home by a little after noon. Mom was forced to listen to my tale of adventure and then I hit the chores. I felt really great and was already figuring how to spend that six dollars I had earned in the great outdoors. By fall I'd be rich!

For the next week I repeated my chub run every other day. Dad usually went through about four dozen chubs every day he guided, so by catchin' eight to ten dozen every other day, I was keepin' ahead of him. The surplus was kept in our own private minnow box, which was built in a spring hole just down the road from our resort at the edge of The Minnow Pond Swamp. This was turnin' out to be the best deal ever! Dad was gettin' the freshest choice chubs and I was gettin' rich! And havin' fun doin' it! And then that old trout butted in.

It happened about the fifth or sixth time I was chubin'. The weather had turned cold and cloudy with a raw northwest wind. June does that once in a while. For some unexplained reason the chubs had seemed to disappear. Oh, I caught a few here and there, but most of the spots where I had been finding lots of chubs, only contained a few. I took a break, sat on the bank, and munched down a Butterfinger candy bar I had stashed in my hip pocket. I began to ponder the puzzling mystery. Where in the heck had those chubs went? And by the time I had licked the last of the chocolate off the wrapper, I thought I had figured out where the chubs were hiding. After all, how smart could a chub be anyhow?

I figured if they weren't in the shallow, slack water, they must be ganged up in the deeper holes. I mean, where else could they be? I gave my hunch a try.

With my best slow sneak, and a minimum of stumblin', I eased up to a nice dark, deep hole protected by an ancient cedar log, that was hung up just under the rippling surface. I tried to drift my little hook and worm into the hole, but the current was too swift for my little BB sized sinker. A check of my hook box located a larger sinker. I squeezed it on the gut leaded with my teeth and tossed the rig back in the hole. I lowered the tip of my cane pole a couple of feet to let that chunk of worm really get down deep where those chubs must be hidin'.

"WHAM!" Something just about jerked the pole out of my hands! I yanked back from instinct, and my eyes nearly popped out of my head when I saw what was hanging on the end of my line! A brook trout about a foot long was thrashing away, trying to give me the slip. And dang it, he did! My little hook was too small to hold in his jaw.

I stood looking into that black hole, where the escaped trout had zoomed, with an expression on my face that would have stopped a clock. Then I yelled a couple of words I'd never dared say if Dad or Mom had been around. Next I almost cried. I'd never caught a trout that big before, in fact I hadn't ever caught a trout of any size before. And this monster was way bigger than most of the ones Dad brought back home for us to eat. My hands started to shake. I had caught the fever!

In the next bend, in the next hole, I lost another trout. This one was only an eight or nine incher, but the same thing happened. The hook just didn't hold. Then it happened two more times in the next two holes. Boy, was I getting mad! Couldn't catch no chubs and those dandy trout were all getting away. But then the light bulb in my head went "On".

My face lit up in devilish grin as I sat on the bank and opened my little box of spare hooks and sinkers. Sure enough! There was a size six hook mixed in with those tiny sized twelve's. In a minute the new hook was tied on the end of the gut leader and a gob of worms replaced the tiny piece I

17

used for chubs. I eased up to hole number five and gently tossed in my new rig.

"WHAM!" This time I was ready. I jerked back and firmly set the hook in my first brook trout! I really didn't give him much of a chance to fight, as I horsed him out of the hole and flung his wiggling body into the knee high grass on the bank. And then I dove on top of him!

I grabbed him in both hands, got a firm grip with my left, and removed the hook. I snapped his neck, as Dad had taught me, and laid his quivering body on the lush green grass. It was a male, as his jutting lower jaw clearly indicated. I stared at him, not quite believing what I had just accomplished. His red spots, outlined in blue, were just short of dazzling. Pale white spots were interspersed with the red and blue ones all along his back and sides. The leading edge of each fin was pure white, standing our distinctly against the darker back portion. And like all brook trout, he had the unmistakable "worm pattern" all over his back. What a beautiful thing he was! And he was all mine! I had outwitted a wily brook trout all by myself! Suddenly, fishing for chubs was kid stuff. I had become a trout fisherman!

By the time I reached Highway C, my minnow bucket contained about a dozen and a half chubs and six trout. I carried the trout home on a forked stick, just like Tom Sawyer and Huckleberry Finn did. And this time Mom was forced to listen to a REAL story!

I finished my chores and watched the hands of the clock creep towards six. Dad would be home about then. I wondered what he's say when he learned his son had become an expert at catching brook trout! The afternoon dragged.

It was a few minutes before six when I heard the engine of Dad's truck laboring up the old dirt road that led from our minnow box to our home. I raced towards the garage where Dad always parked his truck and his Thompson Guide Boat inside, to keep the boat dry in case of rain. I was fairly bursting with pride and couldn't wait to tell him about his son's new found skill.

Dad saw me running across the yard to meet him and gave me his usual friendly smile as he backed the truck and boat into the dry interior of our garage. But he gave me a second look that didn't look quite normal.

"Hi Dad", I greeted. "How'd the fish bite today?"

"Oh, It was slow. That northwest wind pretty much shut them off. We had to work real hard for seven walleyes and a couple of small northern."

"Well, the chubs took the day off too. I only got a few."

"Ya, I noticed the bucket was kinda light. What happened?"

"The chubs weren't in the slack water like they usually are. So I tried the deeper holes. And guess what!! I CAUGHT SIX TROUT!"

"Six trout! How did you manage to catch six trout?"

"Well, I lost the first four that hit, cause my chub hook was too small. But then I put on a size six and a heavier sinker and caught the next six that hit! Sorry I only got a few chubs. BUT CATCHIN' TROUT IS A LOT MORE FUN!"

"Buckshot, I figured you stumble onto catching some trout sooner or later, but I didn't expect it would happen so soon. I suppose I better tell Old Joe to start savin' me some minnows."

Well, my chub catchin' days were over. The trout fishing fever had set in for good. Over the years, till I started going to college and also got booked into a lot of guiding dates during the summer, good old Plum Crick gave up some fine catches of native brook trout. Yes sir, the Anderson Family ate real good.

Later, the Department of Natural Resources decided to plant German Brown trout in Plum Creek. And that idea pretty much ruined the good brook trout fishery. The DNR often forgets, "If it ain't broke, don't fix it." But even this story has a happy ending. Just recently, the stocking of German Brown ended and the native brook trout are thriving once again!

And one additional footnote to my last day as a chub fishermen. It took me a few year to realize that Dad had given me one heck of a nice complement when he resigned himself to the fact I had become a trout fisherman. In fact, it was one of the best compliments I ever got!

# Buck Fever

It had been one of the mildest falls Dad Anderson could remember. Even when deer season rolled around in mid November, the usually snowy forests of northern Wisconsin were still dressed in the drab browns and yellows of late fall. Temperatures during the day were so balmy, even a skinny kid could play out of doors with only one layer of long johns under his overalls. Dad decided the time was ripe to "take the kid on a deer hunt."

Even at age twelve, I could recall lots of good news that had already fallen my way at such a pip squeak age. But this was the top of the pile! A deer hunt!

I'd been allowed to hang around the hunting shack with "the gang" since I had shed my diapers, just waiting for the magical moment when I'd be deemed old and mature enough to get to go on an honest to God deer hunt. At first, I thought Dad was doing some good natured kidding about taking me hunting with him, but Dad Anderson, although he did kid around a lot, didn't kid around about important stuff like huntin' and fishin'. No sir, I could tell by the grin on his weather beaten ruddy red face he was plumb serious!

I think I stood in the kitchen with my mouth hanging open for several minutes till Dad asked, "Well, are you going to stand around looking like your feet are nailed to the floor, or are you going to get your hunting stuff on so we can get going before dark?" I was ready in about two minutes!

It was the day after Thanksgiving. School was closed in honor of the occasion, and all but a couple of the regular members of "the gang" had already filled their tags and departed for their respective homes. The hundreds of acres of forest lands that surrounded our home was devoid of hunters.

Dad stuffed his faithful Winchester lever action model 94, .30-30 under the crook of his arm and ambled westward down our driveway towards his chosen destination. I tagged along behind, toting my new double barreled Stevens model 311, 20 gauge shotgun. I tried my best to mimic Dad's style, but fell far short. My heart was pounding so hard I was sure our nearest neighbors, a full half mile away, could hear it!

A half hour of leisurely walking brought us to a jack pine thicket which flanked one of "the gang's" popular deer hunting areas. The Big Ravine. The ravine had been carved by the flow of water from the ice that melted as the last continental glacier began receding some ten thousand years ago. Once a mighty river, the rushing water had gouged out a fairly straight valley that started several miles north of our location and meandered south

20

for another mile and a half. Here it intersected with another stream which is still active, Plum Creek.

Both ridges on either side of the ravine were covered with modest second growth aspen and jack pine. The lumberjacks had taken everything else thirty years earlier. The landscape was criss crossed with dozens of deer trails. We were right in the middle of the mightiest deer heard the north central area of Wisconsin had ever housed! And today, it all belonged to Dad and me!

Dad's plan of action was simple. He probably kept it that way, considering who his hunting partner was on this memorable afternoon. In low toned whispers, I was instructed to climb up on an ancient fire blackened pine stump and wait for Dad to make a circle along the far side of the ravine. He reasoned some deer should be taking an afternoon nap in the thickets that flanked the open ravine, and his meanderings would set them into motion. Generally, spooked deer would cross the ravine to put some distance between themselves and the human who had interrupted their mid day siesta.

The plan sounded fine to me, and the eternal optimism of youth began to imagine the gigantic buck that would surely choose the very runway that passed within twenty yards of where I stood!

Final instructions were whispered. "O.K. Buckshot, load up and look sharp. Don't go wigglin' and squirmin' on top of that stump, or even a dumb fawn will see you before you see them. If a buck comes down that runway over there, wait till he stops and takes a look back over his shoulder to see if I'm followin' him. Put that front bead right on the widest part of him and touch her off. I'll probably only be gone an hour or so. And stay put! I want to see you on top of this stump when I poke my head out of those jack pines over there."

He gave me one of his most infectious grins and added, "Good luck Buckshot!" In seconds, without so much as a swish of a dead fern or the crack of a dry twig, the forest had swallowed him up. I was all alone in heaven!

I dropped two slugs into the chambers of my little 20 gauge and thought, "O.K. Mr. Buck, I'm ready! Come my way and you'll be as dead as last winters ashes." Such are the dreams of youth!

The woods that November afternoon was the most wonderful place on the face of the earth! I don't believe I had ever felt such joy and happiness. Well, maybe it was a tie with last Christmas when Uncle Bud had hid this little 20 gauge under the tree with my name on the package. Actually, he had broken the gun down into three parts, barrels, stock and receiver, and forearm. Then he made three packages out of it so I wouldn't be able to tell it was a shotgun by looking at a package. His little trick had worked too. I even cried a few small tears of happiness when I ripped off the wrapping and discovered the treasure it had concealed. Next to Mom and Dad, Uncle Bud was the best person in the world. And he was almost like having a second dad.

Minutes ticked by. My imagination conjured up monster buck after monster buck that strolled by my stump. Each one stopped and looked back over his shoulder, just like Dad said they would. The pile of imaginary dead bucks grew larger and larger as my imagination grew wilder and wilder. (It's funny in a way, that every though over fifty deer seasons have passed, my imagination still conjures up those monster bucks. Maybe there's really not much difference between a boy and a man.)

Time dragged on. It felt like I had been standing on that old pine stump for hours. Doubts began to filter into my imagination between the continuing parade of giant bucks. Maybe Dad got lost! Maybe he couldn't remember where he had posted me! Maybe it will get dark soon! Oh God, no, don't let me be left out here in the dark! But I bravely fought back such notions. Why heck, my Dad was the best woodsman since Daniel Boone. He'd be back for me in no time. I felt better.

I had been left alone for perhaps a little better than a half hour. Even though to a twelve year old, it seemed much longer. My attention span had about reached the end of its watching for deer rope. I started looking at chickadees, blue jays, ravens, red squirrels and the such. But the slight snapping of a dry twig brought my senses back to what I was there for.

During my lapse of concentration, I had rotated my body on top of the stump so my back was facing the jack pines from where a deer would appear. Real smart! I slowly turned my head in the direction of the noise I had heard, fully expecting to see Dad returning. But what I saw nearly made my eyes pop out of their sockets!

A magnificent six point buck was slowly walking down the runway I was guarding! And what a sight he was! With his sleek dark brown winter coat and a wide ring of white hair separating the brown hairs from his shinny black nose, he was the best looking deer I had ever seen! He hadn't seen or scented me as of yet and looked so much like a gentleman out for a leisurely afternoon stroll.

My heart beat increased by ten, and leaped into my throat! The palms of my hands, which had been feeling a little like a clam in cold water, began to sweat. I was totally out of position to raise my gun into firing position. My mind bean to scold my body for being 180 degrees off course. But then the buck did just what Dad said he'd do. He stopped and looked back over his shoulder!

I had never shot a slug out of my little 20 gauge, but my mind was quick to recount stories I had listened to in the huntin' shack by members of "the gang" who shot slug guns. Many of the stories had included mention of how fast a slug drops when fired, and often how it was necessary to hold your sight just above the back of a buck when he was a long way off. And to this rookie deer hunter, this buck looked a long way off.

The buck kept looking back over his shoulder long enough for me to ease myself back into shooting position. I shouldered my shotgun, aimed at the widest part of his body, hesitated and then lifted the barrels so that my front bead was just over his back. And then I jerked the front trigger.

The recoil nearly took me off the stump. I staggered around to keep my balance and watched the buck, who had been standing about thirty yards from my point of ambush, go from zero to sixty in one bound! My second slug probably hit something in the next county or perhaps took a chunk out of a low flying cloud. I had no idea where I tried to aim the second shot. I guess I just pulled the back trigger. I had been so surprised the buck hadn't dropped on the spot, like the movies showed when something or somebody got shot, my second shot was pure reaction.

In a split second my buck was gone! My heart left my throat and dropped to the bottom of my stomach. Even at age twelve, I had enough knowledge about hunting to know I had missed.

Dad had let me tag along deer hunting with him on several occasions, just as an observer, you understand. One thing I did learn was that deer, or many other species of game, don't always drop dead when stuck by a bullet or a load of fine shot. But if they are hit, deer usually leave behind some hair and blood. Even though I was positive I had missed, hunting ethics dictated I had to look.

As I dejectedly walked to the location the buck had occupied when I had loosed a three quarter ounce lead projectile at him, the knot in my interior grew larger and harder. I knew I had missed a golden opportunity to bag a nice buck on my first real deer hunt. The soaring joy I had felt less than an hour ago had changed to gloom and despair. Plus, what would Dad say? I'd probably be the laughing stock of the hunting shack for years to come. My high flying spirits of earlier had suddenly plunged to the utmost depth of depression.

I was in the act of half heartedly searching for blood and hair when I head Dad's voice. "Well, how big WAS he?" As usual, Dad had appeared without a sound, and had advanced to within a few yards of where I stood without me even knowing he was about. I jumped several feet in the air and turned to see Dad looking at me with that same infectious grin on his face that he been wearing when he wished me good luck almost an hour ago. Somehow, I never figured out how, but he already knew I had missed.

With lowered eyes and down turned lips, I told Dad exactly what had happened. I had long ago learned it did no earthly good to lie to either parent. They could tell you were going to tell a fib even before you started telling one.

When my tale of woe was completed, I slowly raised my eyes to view Dad's face. It hadn't changed a bit! That beautiful smiling face and twinkling pale blue eyes told me that missing that buck really wasn't a sin after all. The weight in my mid-section relaxed a bit.

Dad put his arm around my shoulders, gave me a little squeeze, and said, "Don't feel bad about missin' one. It's better to miss than wound one and not find him without any trackin' snow. Besides, there's lots of room around them and it's easier to hit thin air rather than what you're aimin' at."

At the time, what he said didn't make a lot of sense to me, although everything Dad tried to teach me made sense. And as usual, it took me a long time to figure it out.

We were back home shortly before dusk. Dad didn't say a word to me all the way home. I was kinda glad he didn't, as I needed the time to think real hard about what had happened and what Dad had told me about missin' that buck.

The warmth of Mom's kitchen, and the smell of fresh baked bread, made the knot in my innards relax a little more. Dad told Mom about our hunt, and again I was glad he did the talkin', as I really didn't feel like reliving that ordeal again so soon, or ever again for that matter. Mom just smiled at me and told me it was no big deal to miss a deer, as we had enough venison to hold us through the winter. She added that I'd get lots more chances to shoot a buck in the years to come. That didn't cheer me up much either. But after a hot supper and a good nights sleep, the defeat I experienced the day before didn't press nearly so hard on my thoughts.

Well, Dad and Mom were right again, as usual. Through the years, and there have been over a half century of them, I've shot lots of bucks and missed a few more. And I've tried to pass on some of that good old home spun wisdom on to my kids and grandkids. And you know what? I really think some of it actually stuck!

# Once Upon The Pine

It was mid March. Nearly all the residents of the north woods were in the depths of severe "cabin fever". The winter had been long and cold and the four walls most people had to look at every day was getting pretty boring. Dad told me God invented March 'cause eternity wasn't long enough. It took me a few years to figure out what that meant. But as usual, Dad was right.

We were having one of those nasty March blizzards. Wet, heavy snow was descending upon the north woods in massive sheets, adding to the three feet that already lay in the forest. The north country was still in the tight fisted grip of Old Man Winter. And Dad said it looked like it might never stop.

To kill some time, which was about the only thing we had plenty of, Dad started telling me stories about when he was a kid, workin' at my grandfather's loggin' camp. Grandpa Anderson had several logging camps over in Forest County along the banks of the Pine River. Dad and his four older brothers all worked in the camps and the stories they told were even better than listening to the Lone Ranger on our battery powered radio.

Well anyway, Dad got into one of his reflective moods and was tellin' me how the loggers used to catch trout out of the beaver flowages to help feed the loggers. They didn't use fish poles, but did real well with dynamite and a few other methods that wasn't legal anymore. And that's a good thing. Not bein' legal anymore I mean. A trout is too nice a fish to get caught with dynamite. After Dad finished his story he got that far away look in his eyes and I knew what was comin' next.

"Buckshot", he started, "this coming spring, if we ever have spring, I'm going to take you over to the Pine and we're going to do some serious trout fishing". And he wasn't thinkin' about usin' dynamite either. "Yes sir", he continued, "we're going to take the tent and spend a couple of days camping where your grandpa had one of his logging camps. And we're going to catch some trout! What do you think of that idea?"

What did I think of that idea? What a dumb question. But I didn't tell Dad I thought it was a dumb question. "WOW", I yelled, "Let's get packed now!" That was a dumb answer. But Dad didn't say it was dumb either. Dad was nice.

The days and weeks and months wore on and finally it was spring. Late May rolled around, ending the misery of school for a few months, and our trip to the Pine started taking shape. I was so excited I could hardly sleep.

Dad had lots of friends, but Charlie was his best buddy. Charlie and his wife moved to the north woods from Chicago shortly after World War II ended, and purchased a resort. Dad and Charlie hit it off real good when they met for the first time at a pinochle table during a winter card party. Dad even got Charlie into doing some guiding during the summer, plus tried to teach him how to hunt grouse, ducks and deer. Charlie seemed to enjoy all that north woods stuff, but he needed lots of practice. Besides, he was left handed. So, Dad nicknamed him "Lefty".

Well, Dad decided he'd take Lefty along with us on our expedition to the Pine and try to teach Charlie all about the fine art of catching trout. That turned out to be a big mistake.

Charlie accepted the invitation and ever offered to us his brand spankin' new 1950 Buick to haul us and all our gear to the Pine. Dad was real surprised that Charlie offered to use his car, 'cause Charlie thought the world of that new Buick and treated it better than a baby. Charlie usually always wanted Dad to use his old Chevy truck when they went huntin' or fishin'. Charlie just didn't know what gettin' to the Pine had in store for his baby!

Early one fine June morning the trio of adventurers headed east on Highway 70 towards the Nicolet National Forest. We turned south on Highway 55 until we crossed the Pine. Dad had Charlie stop his Buick and we all got out for a short history lesson. Dad told us how the 'jacks floated the big pine logs downstream to grandpa's camp. Then the loggers pulled 'um ashore and piled 'um up. "Decked" was the proper word. Later those logs would get loaded on grandpa's very own short spur railroad and hauled to the mills in Leona or Tipler. As I gazed at the slow moving dark water I could just imagine myself riding a raft of big pine logs down the Pine. Suddenly I realized how the river got named! We resumed our journey.

A couple of miles past the Pine, Dad directed Charlie to turn east on a fairly well maintained gravel road. Another mile or so slipped by and Dad told Charlie to slow down to a crawl. Charlie looked puzzled, but eased his new Buick to a bare five miles per hour. Dad kept looking left, out the side window.

"What ya lookin' for?", Charlie inquired.

"The road that used to lead to my dad's old loggin' camp.", Dad answered with a grin.

Charlie kept drivin'. A few hundred yards into our slow crawl, Dad yell for Charlie to stop.

"Here it is!, Dad proclaimed.

"Here's what?, Charlie asked, with a puzzled look on his face.

"The road to the old loggin' camp!", Dad answered.

"What road? I don't see no road." Charlie countered.

Dad pointed. "Right there. See that opening between those two big maples?", Dad directed.

Charlie's eyes got about the size of softballs and looked at Dad in total disbelief. "That's a road? We gotta drive on that? You gotta be out of your mind!"

Well, Dad wasn't kidding and tried to soothe Charlie's growing apprehension. He didn't do too good a job. Charlie was showing signs of panic.

"I can't dive my new car down that trail you call a road! We'll get stuck! The paint will get all scratched up! We'll never make it! I knew we should have taken your truck." Charlie's face looked pale.

Dad told Charlie to quit whinnin' and drive us in. He explained to Charlie that although the road probably hadn't been driven on but a half a dozen times since the early 30's, the 'jacks who built these tote roads always used lots of good gravel and the road bed would be solid. Charlie looked doubtful.

Charlie took another look at Dad's grinning face, put the shift lever in low and let out the clutch. We started creeping towards the Pine. But Charlie's face looked like it was coated with flour.

Tall spring grass and assorted clusters of weeds obscured the faint wheel tracks, as the Buick ground its way slowly towards our intended destination. Dad was chattering away about all his boyhood memories he had gathered here, pointing this way and that to emphasize his ramblings. Dad was enjoyin' himself to the limit! Charlie's face still looked pale.

We were about a quarter mile down the old road when a dry tree limb, which was hidden by the tall grass and weeds, put the first big scratch in the side of Charlie's new green Buick.

"SCREEEECH", went the branch.

"WHAT THE HELL WAS THAT?", screamed Charlie. His face really looked white now.

"Just a little twig rubbing on the side of your car.", said Dad nonchalantly. "Nothin' to worry about."

Charlie stopped his Buick and jumped out to check his baby. "OH MY GOD!", he began. "THAT'S MORE THAN JUST A SCRATCH! THERE'S A DAMN GROVE IN THE DOOR OF MY NEW CAR!"

"It'll buff out", Dad replied. "Let's get going. We've got to get to the Pine and set up camp before it gets dark. And at the rate you're driving, it'll be midnight before we get there." Suddenly Charlie's face was red. I'd never known anybody who could change the color of their face so much, so fast! I thought maybe it was because Charlie was from Chicago.

Another quarter mile crawled by. Suddenly the left front wheel fell into an unseen hole and Charlie's Buick bottomed out. "CRASH, SCRAPE, CLUNK", were the first three sounds we heard. But the "clunk" was followed by a fourth sound, which was the most hideous grinding, whirring, sound ever heard by man. Charlie's face turned white again.

"WHAT THE HELL WAS THAT?" Charlie asked that question a lot in the next couple of days.

Charlie turned off the engine and the noise stopped. We all took turns looking at each other with questioning looks on or faces. Obviously not being mechanics, none of us had the answer to Charlie's question.

We all got out of the car and Charlie opened the hood. Yep, there was an engine. Looked like a normal engine. Didn't seem to be anything out of place, according to Dad and Charlie. Dad offered a suggestion.

"Maybe a stick or something got stuck in the drive shaft and make all that noise. Maybe when you shut off the engine the stick fell out. It sounded like a plausible explanation to me. But the look on Charlie's face said he was skeptical. And his face was red again!

Charlie got back in his car and started the motor. "WHIR, GRIND, WHIR, GRIND", I figured the stick was still stuck in the drive shaft.

"THAT'S MORE THAN A STICK IN MY DRIVE SHAFT!", screamed a crimson faced Charlie. "My car is ruined! I just know it! Why did I ever offer to drive my car on one of your wild adventures. I should have my head examined!"

I couldn't figure out who Charlie thought would examine his head. We were miles from the nearest doctor.

Charlie turned the engine off again and got out of his fairly new Buick. He and Dad talked for a few minutes, trying to decide what should be our next move. Charlie mostly did a lot of hollerin'. Dad was tryin' not to laugh, but wasn't doin' a very good job of it. I guess that was why Charlie's face kept gettin' redder.

I was just standin' way back and wonderin' three things at the same time. One: How were we gonna get out of here if Charlie's Buick was busted? Two: Why is Charlie yellin'? Three: What did Dad find to be so funny? (A couple of years later I figured out the answers to two and three.)

After talkin' and arguin' for a couple of minutes, Dad and Charlie agreed on a plan of action. Charlie would start the car again and either back up or go ahead, whichever the Buick decided it could do, if either. If the car could crawl out of the hole it had found, maybe somebody could crawl under it and try to figure out what was causing the "whir" and "grind" noises.

With Dad and me pushin' we finally got Charlie's rapidly depreciating Buick to move forward. The real wheel also banged through the hole, but we succeeded in getting the injured Buick up on firm, level ground. By then the whirring and grinding was fading away to a tinny "clinking" sound. The mystery deepened.

But there wasn't enough clearance to allow someone to crawl under the car. Another short meeting took place. By now Charlie's face and neck had softened to a light pink. He sure was an amazin' man. Changing from one color to another was sure a remarkable ability.

A new plan emerged. Dad said if we piled a couple of solid logs on a flat rock we could make a ramp. And sure enough, it worked! Charlie slowly moved his sick Buick's left front wheel up the make shift ramp until there was enough clearance for someone to crawl under and check out the damage. I was amazed how adults could be so smart!

Charlie was somewhat thinner than Dad, so he did the crawlin'. Charlie slizzered under his Buick till just his feet were sticking out. There was a silence stiller than death hanging over the area. A minute or two ticked away and finally Charlie spoke.

"I found out what happened!" There was a pause as though Charlie wanted one of us to ask, "What?" He continued. "A big rock must have hit the housing that covers the fly wheel of the clutch assembly and dented it in. The teeth on the fly wheel rubbed on the housing and made all that terrible noise. It rubbed a hole in the housing and that's why the noise has almost gone away. Open the trunk and get out my tool box. I think I can fix her up so we can drive again."

Dad gave me a wink and a grin. In a couple of minutes Dad was handing Charlie a hand full of assorted wrenches and screw drivers. But another problem cropped up.

From under the Buick came Charlie's voice with another request. "Roy", (Charlie always called Dad "Roy" rather than "Andy", which was what everyone else called him.) "I must have dropped my glasses out there somewhere when I bent over to crawl under the car. See if you can find them for me so I can see what I'm doing under here."

Dad took a couple of steps backwards as he stared into the thick grass, his eyes searching for Charlie's missing glasses. Just then a new sound reached our ears. "KER-RUNCH!"

From under the car came, "WHAT THE HELL WAS THAT?"

Dad lifted his left foot and there were Charlie's glasses. Or at least what was left of them. He held them up for me to view. One lens was shattered, but was still in place, being held firmly by the plastic frame. Dad grinned, put his finger to his lips to form the "sssssssshhhh" signal, and loudly proclaimed, "You're in luck Charlie, I found your glasses."

Charlie's hand appeared from under his Buick and Dad laid the broken glasses in it. The hand disappeared.

I would guess about six seconds expired before the explosion. "WHAT HAPPENED TO MY NEW GLASSES? WAS THAT THE KER-KRUNCH I HEARD?"

Dad made the mistake of snickering a bit too loud.

"I DON'T SEE WHAT'S SO (bleeping) FUNNY! YOU(bleep, bleep, bleep)". I was wondering what color Charlie's face was now, but I wasn't willing to crawl under the Buick to find out. There as some things you just have to live without.

In a little less than an hour Charlie had removed the dented housing and used a rock to pound out what remained of the dent. Dad suggested the hole in the housing would probably help keep the fly wheel cooler. However, I don't think his suggestion made Charlie any cooler. Within an hour we were back in the repaired Buick creeping toward the Pine. The color of Charlie's face was almost back to normal.

The remainder of our trip to where the so called road ended was uneventful, except for three or four more minor scratches on the sides of Charlie's recently new Buick. Charlie and Dad were awful quiet, except for a snicker now and then from Dad. I kept wishin' he'd let me in on what was so funny. But a little inner voice told me to keep my mouth shut. I listened too!

Our journey ended about a hundred feet or so from the Pine River. The visible remains of the old raised railroad grade paralleled the river, and its somewhat level surface offered us, what at the time appeared to be a perfect location to pitch our tent. While Dad and Charlie got the tent set up and began to store our gear in it, I was assigned the task of cutting a massive pile of balsam and spruce boughs. These were piled a foot thick on the floor of our tent and made a dandy mattress. Charlie was impressed!

By the time our camp site was ship shape, Old Sol was just starting to kiss the tops of the towering pines and tamaracks good-bye for another day. It was time to catch some trout for supper.

Dad got his fly rod set up first, as usual, pulled on his hip boots, grabbed his net and creel and headed for the river. I was about five minutes behind him.

Evening is the second most beautiful time of day. Morning is a hands down first! I always felt watchin' things wake up and come to life was a bit better than listenin' to things tellin' me they was gettin' ready to go to bed.

The sounds of evening were just starting to orchestrate. A robin was perched high in a birch tree chirping his "I want rain" call. I knew he was out of luck. A high pressure area was right smack dab on top of us. A blue jay "jayed" somewhere in the forest on the far side of the river. A pair of mourning doves "cooed" to each other a bit downstream. Grandfather frog croaked his o.k. for the rest of his clan to harmonize with him. And a dozen or more of Mother Nature's assorted sounds joined in the chorus.

A bit of early evening fog was just beginning to form along the shaded portion of the river bank, when the most unforgettable, sweet sound one will ever hear on the banks of a trout stream began. A white throat sparrow softly chirped out his rendition of the beginning of "Oh Canada". As I stood at the edge of the water listening to Mother Nature providing such wonderful sounds, it seemed almost like a sin that we humans had trespassed into this pristine sanctuary. But then again, I was getting hungry. I waded in and limbered my fly rod.

Dad was upstream in the bend above me casting his fly line, which was making a soft swishing sound, with that ever so easy rhythm he had tried unsuccessfully to teach me. He was poetry in motion. Dad was a magician with a fly rod. I watched him for a minute or two, and then began to beat the water with my favorite fly, a Royal Coachman.

A few small trout were rising to a hatch of May flies at the tail end of the pool I was flailing to a froth with my fly. No luck. I reluctantly changed my coachman to a May fly and resumed frothing the pool. And by the grace of divine intervention I actually hooked and landed a trout. Not a record breaker, but a nice chunky ten inch rainbow. I had my supper.

Trout number two had just entered my creel when I realized Charlie had not yet appeared. I started to get a little worried that something was wrong, again. But then I remembered Charlie was always slow at getting his act together anytime we went out of dooring. Dad said it was either because he came from the city or was left handed, or both. I guess Charlie just thought about what he had to do too much instead of just doing it.

My third trout of the evening had just finished thrashing his last thrash when I heard Charlie stomping down the hill to the river. Twilight had already begun to set in, and Charlie was in a hurry to get in a bit of fishing before full dark. He was about to experience the dangers one might encounter by hurrying into unknown waters.

Looking back on what happened next, I guess it was my fault for not telling Charlie about the giant, flat, slippery rock just under the surface of the river about ten feet from shore. Well, as Charlie came charging into the river, he reminded me of a movie I saw about our Marines rushing ashore at Omaha Beach on D-Day. Then Charlie discovered the rock.

I tried real hard not to laugh, but he sure was funny the way he stubbed his toe on the rock, did a nearly perfect forward flip, and landed with a splash that silenced all God's creatures for a mile in all directions. Dad looked downstream and asked, "WHAT THE HELL WAS THAT?" I couldn't see what color Charlie's face was now, 'cause I was laughing too hard.

As Charlie struggled to his feet, his first remark did nothing to suppress my mirth. "I guess I stumbled on a rock." My laughter intensified to a roar. Dad headed downstream to see what was causing all the ruckus.

31

Dad arrived just after Charlie had dragged his soaked, dripping body out of the river. He was sitting on a stump, pouring water out of one of his hip boots. There were several gallons. Dad took one look at Charlie and knew right off what had happened. Then Dad broke down with uncontrollable laughter. When I vividly described exactly what had happened to Charlie, Dad roared even harder. This time I knew what was so funny. Charlie's face had turned blue.

After Charlie dumped the water out of his other boot, we walked the short distance to our camp. Dad got a blazin' campfire roaring, and Charlie stripped off all his soggy clothes and hung them on forked sticks around the fire to start the dryin' process. Every so often Dad or I would look at Charlie and let out another little giggle. Charlie didn't seem to be able to fine anything funny about the situation. But at least his blue face was gone and it was just pale again.

Besides my three trout, Dad's creel contained five. No surprise there. While I went back to the river to clean our catch, Dad set up his Coleman gas stove and started frying some potatoes and heating up a can of beans. Charlie just sat close to the fire and kinda shivered. His face looked red again, but I guess it was just the reflection from the fire.

Supper was the best ever. Fresh trout fried up in a little butter over a low flame, a pile of crispy French fries, a mound of baked beans, and a couple of slices of Mom's homemade bread, made a meal beyond belief. Dad grossed Charlie out a little when he ate a couple of fried trout heads. Dad always ate some trout heads when we had trout for supper. I tied 'um a few times, but the only part of the head I can really say is tasty is the cheek meat. I did eat some cheeks. Charlie passed on both items. And his face looked pale again.

After we cleaned up our mess from supper, Dad fired up his Coleman lantern and we retired to our tent. Although it was only nine thirty, we were plenty tired. It was too bad we didn't get much sleep.

We had no more than turned off the lantern and rolled up in our blankets on that mattress of soft, fragrant boughs, when Charlie made an announcement.

"SOMETHING IS CRAWLING ON ME!" And then his flashlight flashed on.

Well, about that time, I thought I felt something crawling on me. Dad agreed, he too felt something crawling on him. By now there were three flashlights turned on. And we discovered the crawling sensation was not our imaginations! All three of us were infested with wood ticks!

Dad re-lit his Coleman lantern and the tent blazed with yellow brightness. As our eyes grew accustomed to the bright light, we beheld an awesome spectacle. Wood ticks were everywhere! The tent contained dozens, maybe hundreds! Charlie had another announcement.

"AAAAAAAAHHHHHHHHHH!!!!!" I figured bein' from the city, Charlie was pretty excited about seein' so many wood ticks in one place, not to mention the fact that several dozen were crawlin' around on various parts of his body. Charlie musta thought we hadn't heard his first, "AAAAAAAAHHHHHHHH", 'cause he did again.

"AAAAAAAAAHHHHHHHHHHHH!!!!" It was a little louder this time. In fact, all the night sounds we had been hearin' stopped. Charlie's face was back to pale.

Dad went outside and returned to the tent carrying a bucket with about an inch of water in the bottom. For the next half hour or so we sat in kinda a rough circle and picked wood ticks off each other. Then we'd drop 'um into the bucket to see if they could swim. They could, but not for very long.

After our bodies seemed free of ticks, we picked a few more dozen off the walls of the tent and sent them to Davy Jones' Locker. The bottom of the bucket was covered with them! Dad figured they must have been in the balsam and spruce boughs, so we gathered them all up and tossed them out of our tent. After rolling up in our blankets once more, we discovered there were a nice batch of good sized rocks under the floor of our tent. So each of us began to roll and squirm, trying to find a flat spot so we might get back to sleep. It wouldn't have done much good, because the next night time episode was about to begin!

"SMACK!" Something that sounded about the size of Charlie's Buick hit the side of our tent right by Charlie's ear. "WHAT THE HELL WAS THAT?" I think all of us probably said the same thing in unison. Three flashlight once again blazed as one. My eyes felt like they were going to pop out of my head. Charlie's had eyes that make him look like Eddie Cantor, and even Dad's eyes were a tad larger than normal.

"SMACK!" That something smacked our tent again! I looked at Dad, hoping for a simple explanation. He was holding an ax and looking at the door of our tent as though he expected something to barge in on us. I think this was the only time in my life I remember Dad looking a little scared.

We all sat in frozen silence, waiting for that unseen something to rip a hole in our tent and start using us for a night time snack. An eternity seemed to pass, although it was probably only a few seconds, when Dad, ax and flashlight in hand, opened the tent flap and stepped out into the unknown darkness. I was ready to wet my blankets! Charlie's face looked like something you'd see in a wax museum.

We could hear Dad pokin' around outside where the unknown somethin' had whacked our tent. I expected to hear him scream, or that unknown somethin' let out a blood chillin' growl, or Dad's bones breakin' or some other hideous sound. But what we heard was Dad's deep belly laugh. Charlie finally blinked.

"You'll never guess what was smackin' the side of our tent!" There was a pause, as though Dad was waiting for one of us to ask, "What?" Dad continued. "We pitched our tent right on a major rabbit runway and the darn critters are trying to race over the top of the old railroad grade and are smackin' into our tent. HAR DE HAR HAR HAR"

As of yet, neither Charlie or I could figure out what was so funny. But we did both sigh a sigh of relief!

Moving the tent was too big a job in the dark, so we just rolled up in our blankets again, tried unsuccessfully to find a level spot between the rocks, and listened to rabbits thumping against the sides of our tent till daybreak. Several times Charlie mumbled somethin' about the genetic defects in rabbits and slandered their ethnic backgrounds quite liberally. I think that was the longest night I ever experienced.

Dad cooked us a great breakfast of fried eggs, crisp bacon, more fried potatoes, and boilin' hot coffee, along with more of Mom's homemade bread. I even tried some coffee. It tasted terrible, but it's warmth felt real good on my innards.

After breakfast, Dad and I fished a couple of hours and caught a few more trout to take home for Mom and Uncle Bud. Charlie's hip boots were still cold and clammy wet, so he just sat on the bank of the river and smoked one of his nickel William Penn cigars to keep the mosquitoes away.

Dad told Charlie that he had named that big old flat rock, "Charlie's Rock". Charlie responded with somethin' I wasn't quite able to make out. But the jist of his reply was that he told Dad to move the rock someplace else. That was the part I didn't hear. Exactly where he'd like Dad to move the rock. Actually, "Shove it" was part of the phrase I head. Well, Dad didn't even try to move that old rock. It would have been way too heavy.

About noon we broke camp and loaded all our gear back into Charlie's Buick for the return trip. Charlie had walked all the way out to the main road and busted off all the twigs and sticks that had scratched his baby on the way in. So he didn't add any scratches on the way out. He was even able to avoid the big hole that dented his fly wheel housing! Charlie had sure learned how to drive on those so called roads in one easy lesson.

None of us said much on the two hour drive back home. I guess we were all too tired. Dad did ask Charlie if he'd had a good tune, Charlie looked at Dad, then looked over his shoulder at me in the back seat, and didn't answer. I guess he had to think about it for a spell before he make up his mind. It musta took a lot of thinkin', as he never did answer Dad's question.

But I did see the back of his neck turn red.

# Doubles On Grouse Are Easy, If You Have A Good Dog

"Hey Dad, I've got all my chores done. Can we go huntin'?" Dad heard that question for the past several years during most of September, October and November. During May through August the question had been, "Can we go fishin'?"

I suspected what his answer would be. And I was right. "Buckshot, you know I'd love to go with you, but, well, there is still a big pile of logs on the skid-way at our mill, and me and Uncle Bud have to get them sawed up real soon, as another truck load will be arrivin' in a couple of days." Mom, Dad and Uncle Bud always had a lot of work to do.

I kinda felt sorry for them lots of times. Seemed like they never had much extra time to just do whatever they wanted, like kids can. Work always seemed to get in the way. I had a tough time figurin' that out too. My history book, which I was forced to read in school, said the Great Depression was over by about 1940. I guess those historians didn't know about northern Wisconsin, where Depression existed in great abundance well into the 1950's.

Dad went over my list of chores to make sure I hadn't missed any.

"Wood box filled?"

"Yep."

"Fresh ice in the ice box?"

"Yep."

"Kindling split?"

"Yep."

"All the sawdust that was in the pit under the saw at the mill hauled away?"

"Yep."

"Garbage hauled out of the kitchen?"

"Yep."

"Did you ask the Admiral if she needs you to do anything else?"

"Yep."

"Did she?"

"Nope."

"Then you better get Old Pat and see if you can shoot your mother a couple of grouse. She likes that white meat, and is getting a little tired of venison, duck, rabbit and salt pork."

"THANKS DAD!"

Old Pat was our black cocker spaniel. He was one of the huntin'est dogs you ever did see. Dad called him "a dog for all seasons." Once he figured out what it was you were after, he was all business. If it was a grouse you

35

needed, he'd find a grouse. If I felt like shootin' a snowshoe, he'd chase the hares out of their hidin' spots and let me shoot one. If you blasted a mallard or wood duck down on the crick, he's swim out and get 'um. If you had a cripple hidin' in the weeds, he'd find 'um. His only drawback was bein' bullheaded. Mom said all males are like that. Guess she was mostly right.

The world that sunny early October afternoon was all mine. Our one hundred and twenty acres was bordered by another hundred and twenty, which was owned by tourists from Illinois. They usually were only around their cottage for a few weeks in the summer. Dad and Uncle Bud were their caretakers, and we had full run on their land to hunt or trap or cut any dead trees for firewood. Within this two hundred and forty acres of my private domain rested Dollar Lake, although we referred to it simply as "The Lake". To have all this wild beauty to roam on made me a very lucky thirteen year old. And I was slowly beginning to realize it.

My hunting plan, if I were so bold to call what I did a plan, was simple and one I had used many times in my short life span. I'd follow the old dirt road that passed the sawmill, swing right where it forked towards Lost Crick, and continue on this two rut road to The Lake. That's were the Illinois tourists had their cottage. Next, I'd follow the east shoreline south, then west, and then north back to our home. That'd take about two hours. But if I decided to make a detour to "The Pot Hole" in Franke's Swamp to see if any ducks were resting on it, well that'd take another hour. Seeing the day was young, and so was I, the side trip to The Pot Hole sounded like a good bet.

Dad and Uncle Bud were sawin' away on that never ending pile of pine logs when I walked past the mill. They gave me and Old Pat a wave and a grin to wish us a bit of good luck. I felt a little guilty that I was going on another adventure, while they were slaving away at that noisy old mill. But somebody had to get Mom a couple of grouse, and I had been elected!

A bit past the sawmill the road creased the edge of The Minnow Pond Swamp. Here Dad and Uncle Bud had dug some ponds with picks and shovels. The ponds filled with ice cold spring water, which gurgled upward in abundance, and Dad used these ponds to stockpile minnows he caught. We sold a few to tourists and Dad used the rest himself when he guided fishermen. Sometimes ducks visited this quiet retreat.

Old Pat was racing ahead, still not sure of what his master was hunting on this fine fall afternoon, and flushed a pair of wood ducks out of the alders that shaded Dad's minnow ponds. I pulled up my little 20 gauge double, but held back as the woodies were a mite out of range. Old Pat gave me a look that would freeze boilin' water. I pretended I hadn't seen the ducks. Old Pat didn't believe me. Our next destination was Lost Crick.

Right where the old dirt road first reaches the crick I had brushed out a nice sneakin' trail, which would silently led me to a wide, shallow, weedy bend in the river. There were usually a few mallards or wood ducks feeding there, or simply resting. I used Dad's wheelbarrow to haul sawdust from his mill to pave the trail so I could sneak up to the crick without makin' a sound. Dad could do that without sawdust, but I hadn't mastered that skill yet. I needed lots of sawdust. The bend of the crick contained one blue heron and a lazy muskrat.

About half way from the crick to The Lake, Old Pat treed a noisy red squirrel. Pat gave a couple of yips to let me know he had one of those pesky critters up a tree. But 20 gauge shells were just too expensive to waste blasting a poor little red squirrel, and I told Pat so. This time he believed me.

There weren't any ducks on The Lake either. I guess it was just too nice of an afternoon. I took a break from the hunt and sat on a log, just looking out on the sparkling blue water. Our resident loons hadn't headed south yet, as I could see them silently diving out in the middle of the lake, probably catching little perch for a snack.

West, down the north shore of The Lake, I could see our dock, about a quarter of a mile away. Boy, had I caught a lot of fish off that dock! While I was resting and doing a little daydreaming, Old Pat took a swim and lapped up about a gallon of cool. clean water to cool off. He had already put on a few miles of zig zaggin', tryin' to find somethin' I could blast away at. In a couple of minutes Old Pat came ashore, shook some water out of his long black hair, and gave me his "Let's get huntin'" look. It was time to move on.

A well worn deer path angled away from The Lake and passed over a small ridge that separated The Lake from Franke's Swamp. The deer path would led me to The Pot Hole, which was smack dab in the middle of the swamp.

As swamps go, this one was one of my favorites. About sixty acres in size, it was covered with black spruce trees that grew thicker than Mom's pea soup. In winter time, snowshoe hares lived in the swamp in countless numbers, creating well packed trails in the deep snow that were a foot wide and just as deep. During deer season, the gang that stayed at our resort always pushed a couple of nice bucks out of this swamp. And even a grouse or two might pop up in the thickets when they'd been flushed off the high ground or were lookin' for a nice cool spot to hole up during the heat of the day. But best of all was The Pot Hole, an oasis of beauty in the midst of beauty.

I first found out about The Pot Hole when I was just a young kid, about eight. Dad, Mom and Grandma Jorgensen harvested wild cranberries on the banks of the little bog lake. A person had to be darn careful too, as the whole shoreline was one of those floating bogs. If somebody got careless, they might fall through a beaver hole in the bog and never get out! At least that's what Dad told me. And I believed him, 'cause once I fell in one of those beaver holes when we were pickin' cranberries and Dad had to drag me out! It sure wasn't much fun, fallin' in I mean. When you got pulled out you were covered with the stinkin'est, slimiest goo and muck you ever did smell. Worst than a rotten skunk!

Well anyway, I discovered ducks also liked to nibble on those little sour wild cranberries, or sometimes just dropped down on that secluded pot hole to rest. Usually I checked out The Pot Hole at least once a week during duck season. Sometimes more often.

The walk through the spruce thickets was cool and refreshing, but the surface of The Pot Hole was as empty as the bright blue sky above. A few sickly looking lily pads floated quietly along the bank, but not even a little painted turtle could be seen on any of the logs they usually lined up on to catch some afternoon sun. Old Pat looked disgusted. We were now nearly seventy five percent of the way through our hunt and the kid hadn't had a feather to shoot at. At least not yet. We move on.

We emerged from the swamp, re-crossed the small ridge, and continued following the high ground which overlooked the south shore of The Lake. And then it happened!

Old Pat suddenly stuck his nose about two inches deep in the dry leaves, took a sniff that sounded like the suction of an old vacuum cleaner, and turned his stub tail into high gear. He was definitely on the hot scent of a grouse!

I followed his meandering sniffing for perhaps twenty yards, when suddenly a brown ball of feathers, trailing a tail of fanned gray feathers, exploded from a clump of dead ferns. I knew how grouse can scare the dickens out of you when they unexpectedly burst from cover, as they had nearly made me soil my britches more than once. But somehow they can still cause your heart to skip a couple of beats even when you expect one is going to roar skyward.

Even under the best conditions, there never seems to be enough time to get off a well aimed shot when a grouse takes wing. When they surprise you and roar off, it's often wiser to just not shoot and save your expensive shells. So my outdoor teacher, Dad Anderson, told me to "Shoot at 'um from instinct." Whatever that meant. This October afternoon I was about to understand what he was talking about.

My little 20 gauge was coming to my shoulder as the grouse began to level off, for what would surely be another zig zag flight through the popples to safety. I had probably shot at a dozen or so when they were busting from cover, and the grouse had achieved a 100% successful escape record. My young mind was positive the only way to hit one of those feathered rockets was to pop them while they were sitting on an old log or clinging to the limb of a tree, BEFORE they took wing.

The departing grouse was just starting its first aerial maneuver, which was a sharp bank to the left, when I unloosed an ounce of number seven and a half's, on what I later guessed was "instinct". Then, it what at the time seemed to happen in slow motion, the air was filled with a puff of brown feathers, the grouse folded up like a deflated football, and fell stone cold dead unto a beautiful carpet of colored leaves!

The roar of my little 20 hadn't even died in my ears when another familiar sound exploded just to my left. A second grouse was up and humming through the popples, heading for Franke's Swamp. I swung the barrels of my shotgun towards his departing shape and touched off my second barrel in its general direction. Later I determined my second shot was pure "instinct" too. The grouse set it's wings and sailed out of sight over the ridge I had just crossed.

Old Pat found the first grouse I had somehow miraculously killed, and was in the act of retrieving it to me when I fired at grouse number two. At the sound of my second shot, Old Pat dropped the first grouse and raced off in the direction where he had last seen grouse number two departing. I yelled at him to stop, but as I said earlier, his one negative quality was being bullheaded. He didn't stop.

I picked up my first "shot on the wing" grouse. Over and over I thought, "I really can kill them on the fly!" I knew it could be done, as I'd seen Dad do it dozens of times. But then again, he KNEW all about shooting from instinct.

I sat down on a cushion of colored leaves and leaned against the base of a popple tree. And then I admired my grouse and new found skill at killing them on the fly. A couple of minutes passed before I realized Old Pat was still missing. Where in the heck was that old bullhead. I called. No dog. I called again. Still no dog. I was about to start walking back towards Franke's Swamp to look for him when I heard him running in the dry leaves.

Old Pat was just cresting the top of the ridge, with his long ears a floppin' like he was a bird tryin' to take off. And then I saw he was carrying something in his mouth. Something brown and feathery. What in the world had that old dog found now?

Within seconds Old Pat was by my side. Besides the dead grouse in his mouth his face contained a grin a mile wide! He dropped the second bird at my feet as professionally as any blue ribbon field champion that ever sniffed a scent. My mind finally comprehended what had happened!

A couple of my stray seven and a half's had found their target. The grouse's flight plan, and remaining energy, had been enough to sail over the ridge and out of my sight before he crash landed and died. Old Pat, somehow, instinct maybe, had kept a lookin' and kept a sniffin' till he found that dead bird. He knew who had shot it, and he knew that's where he had to fetch it. I told you earlier, Old Pat was one of the huntin'est dogs you ever saw!

I guess I stood around for five minutes tellin' Old Pat he was the best dern bird dog there ever was, and at the same time I gave his head about two dozen love pats. He just sat by my feet, huffin' and puffin' with that grin still on his face, and lovin' every minute of it. Dogs like that kind of stuff. So do kids.

I finally stuffed both grouse in my·game pouch and took Old Pat down the hill to The Lake so he could cool off with another swim and lap up another gallon of water. He enjoyed that too. Then we hightailed it for home!

I suppose, looking back on what happened that wonderful October afternoon, Old Pat probably wondered why I just about broke the sound barrier heading home. There was still nearly a half mile of good woods to hunt and plenty of time to do it before sundown. But even a wise old dog like Pat didn't know how much I needed to tell Dad, Mom and Uncle Bud my amazing story!

Old Pat and me were still a quarter mile from home when I heard the sound of the sawmill still buzzin' through those piles of pine logs. So I knew right where I could find Dad and Uncle Bud.

I guess the look on my face gave part of my story away before I even got clean around the skid-way full of logs. Dad spotted Old Pat first and knew I wouldn't be far behind. So he was looking for me when I rounded the end of the skid-way. He was reaching for the shut off switch before I even stated reaching into my game pouch to show him my "double" on FLYING grouse! I think I told you before, my Dad was pretty smart.

Both listeners sat down on a pile of fresh sawed pine boards and let the kid pour out his story. I can still see the smirks on their faces and smell the delightful fragrance of fresh sawed pine. When I finished the entire tale, both Dad and Uncle Bud shook my hand and gave me a pat on the back! I felt almost growed up.

"Well Buckshot", Dad began, "Get those two grouse cleaned and deliver 'um to your mother. She'll be darn happy to take them off your hands, AFTER they're cleaned. Then put on your work clothes and get back here as soon as you can. As you can see, the pit under the saw if almost full of sawdust." I grinned my best grin and headed for the fish and game cleaning room next to our icehouse.

I made Mom listen to my tale of adventure, and although she seemed to be real interested, I'm not so sure she was. But those two nice plump grouse did interest her real much! I'd get to nibble on the legs when Mom cooked 'um, 'cause Mom only liked the white meat. She said the legs had too many tendons and gristle. I wasn't fussy. I'd chomp 'um down, tendons and all!

Thinking back on the whole situation, I guess Dad, Mom and Uncle Bud were probably happier for me than I was. Although maybe not. As the years passed, and I somehow got a tad bit smarter, I realized that joy and happiness is often easier to give to someone else than it is to get yourself. And the sight of seeing your children or grandchildren learn, grow and mature is one of life's most joyful gifts.

I was glad that I was given the opportunities to give something back!

# It Was Devine For Ducks

For people who aren't normal, I mean those who don't fish or hunt or camp or do other kinds of outdoor stuff, tryin' to figure out what we outdoor enthusiasts do in the land of Mother Nature is beyond impossible. Those non-normal folks, the ones who have never given the outdoor life a try, just can't understand what we outdoor lovers love about the out of doors! Some of 'um even think those of us who worship the woods and water are one pint short of a quart. And thinkin' thoughts like that is just like a kid saying they don't like green beans, and yet have never tried green beans. I love green beans!

What I'm tryin' to say is this. Why don't those folks who try to take away or restrict what we out of doors enthusiasts get enjoyment from just mind their own business and leave us alone? We outdoor sports supporters don't go around tryin' to stop the "anti's" from shoppin' or goin' on vacation to some ritzy place, or whoopin' it up at some black tie party, or whatever. Who cares what they do? So why do so many of them stick their noses into tryin' to restrict or take away our legal enjoyments? Well, that's why Dad said those types ain't normal. And as ususl, he was right!

You might be wonderin' what prompted all this editorializin'. Well, I started thinking about duck huntin'. I don't suppose my explanation offers a clear connection between outdoor "anti's" and ducks. So I guess I better fill in the missing pieces.

Many years ago, when I was about thirteen years old and knew everything about everything, I was chatting with what turned out to be an "anti", who lived in a big city full of crime and pollution. This person happened to be a tourist who was up north for the first time and as they put it, "I'm bored to death!" Somewhere along in our conversation I was asked, "What do you country bumpkins do for excitement in this God forsaken place? And I made the mistake of tellin' her.

I started listin' stuff like fishin' for pike, bass, walleye, trout, musky, pan fish during the spring, summer and early fall. Then I tossed in some ice fishin' in the winter when it's nice and cold and crisp out on the lakes. Then I told her we bumpkins did a lot of huntin' for grouse, rabbits, deer, woodcock, squirrels, and the like. I added a little narrative about how much fun it is followin' a beagle through a snow covered cedar swamp after snowshoe hares. And almost forgot to tell her how much fun it is seining for whitefish and cisco just before the lakes freeze up. Especially on a pitch dark night when the wind is blowin' thirty miles per hour and the snow is flyin'. I really poured on the sweet talk tellin' how much pleasure can be had wadin' a gin clear trout stream fly fishin' for brook trout. And then I finished her off with a good dose of duck huntin'.

Well, when I ran out of listin' stuff, I knew I was in trouble. She asked me why I'd want to hurt all those sweet, innocent, brown eyed creatures. And she was especially upset that I'd actually try to shoot Donald, Daisy, and Huey, Dewey and Louie.

I explained to this young, uninformed, "anti" that all the above mentioned critters don't have brown eyes. She told me eye color didn't matter. At least she was open minded about that.

Then I thought if I vividly described how wonderful, let's say, a duck hunt is, she might just understand why we outdoor lovers get so much enjoyment out of our outdoor adventures. Like a duck hunt! It's fun even if you don't shoot a duck. Or sometimes never ever get a shot at one. And some times we don't even see one. But we still have fun! She said she'd listen.

So I launched into a detailed narrative about how great it is to roll out of bed about four a.m., eat a solid breakfast of cholesterol rich bacon, eggs, buttered toast, whole milk and wash it all down with black coffee. Next, comes pullin' on a batch of heavy wool clothes and a pair of smelly waders. Then, with your faithful retriever sitting next to you in the front seat, panting so hard he fogs up the windshield, drive a few miles to a marsh.

Once at your chosen hunting area, your canoe is removed from your vehicle and packed to overflowing with sacks of decoys, your gun and several boxes of assorted shells, a thermos of hot coffee, a bag of homemade chocolate chip cookies, and a dog that is going bonkers with glee. Now it's time to paddle a mile and a half in the dark. In a cold, driving, rain. Mixed with sleet and snow. I informed her that weather like that is the best for duck hunting because the ducks like to fly in bad weather looking for a place where it isn't bad.

After a half hour of paddling, you find your blind. At this point in my exciting story I had to explain to my listener what a "blind" was. She thought it had something to do with failing eyesight. Next comes putting out the decoys. The best pattern to us is the "J" pattern, better known as the "fish hook".

"Wait a minute," she interrupted, "I thought you were going duck hunting, not fishing."

After I straightened her out on that point, I mentioned putting out a few dozen decoys had to be done with bare hands, even in freezing weather. That's because the strings and weights used to anchor the decoys are always tangled up. Untangling the decoy strings is usually done in the dark, as either you forgot your flashlight in your vehicle, the batteries are dead, or you dropped it in the water and it won't work.

Once decoys are arranged just right, the canoe is dragged a hundred feet behind your blind and hidden beneath layers of hand picked grass, sticks and clumps of mud. Generally you'll only cut your fingers on the sharp edges of marsh grass two or three times.

After a few minutes of searching for your blind in the dark, and by luck finding it, it's time to relax for the next half hour until legal shooting time, which begins one half hour before sunrise. At this point my audience informed me she had never gotten up early enough to see the sun rise.

First comes a nice cup of hot coffee. Well, it's a nice thought, as the thermos is still in your vehicle. But at least the cookies will taste good. Now where is that bag of cookies, and why is old Duke licking his chops? Oh well, I really didn't need any cookies anyway.

Time seems to drag as shooting time draws near, how near is hard to tell as your wrist watch is still on the dresser at home. So, you have to make a wild guess as to when it's a half hour before sunrise and hope you're right or at least the game warden is still in bed and doesn't hear any too early shots. All game wardens have heard the "I left my watch on my dresser" excuse.

By the time legal shooting time arrives most of your body is numb. But it's good to know that shivering is your bodies way of stimulating blood flow and helping to warm you up.

At last the magical moment arrives! You hear a rush of air over beating wings as a flock of early risers pass over your blind. Cold flesh is quickly replaced by warm goose bumps, as your eyes strain to see through the pre-dawn gloom as to what species of waterfowl have presented you with an awesome fly by. A warm, moist noise nuzzles your hand. Yes, your retriever has heard them also!

It was here in my stirring story that I noticed my "anti" from the city was apparently loosing interest in my duck hunting story. Or, possibly she walked away because she was so brokenhearted for never being invited to go on a real duck hunt. I'll never be sure.

But anyway, when the subject of duck hunting comes up, I get a whole batch of wonderful memories. Some of the best! And many are simply Devine.

I can still vividly recall my first duck hunt. And shooting my first duck. I was eleven. Dad hauled me west of Minocqua and Woodruff to a place called Squaw Creek. It was the opening day of duck season. Legal shooting time on opening day begins at noon. Sometime about mid-afternoon, after Dad had already shot his limit, a flock of blue winged teal buzzed our decoys. Teal generally fly low and fast, with speeds that seem to approach that of military fighter jets.

I'd been well coached about "lead", and "swing" and "follow through", being the proper sequence when shooting at passing ducks. Dad spotted the swift flying teal long before I did and had me all primed and ready when they swooped over our decoys at about mach two. Naturally, I forgot all about my coaching and simply blasted a load of number sixes at the front of the flock. To my surprise, and probably also to the teal, the last bird in the flock folded cleanly and landed in the cat tails "ker-plop", on the other side of the river. At first I thought Dad had fired at the same time I had, but he hadn't.

When Old Pat returned from his retrieve with my first duck, which probably weighed twelve ounces, I couldn't have been happier if it had been a twelve pound goose!

Well, that first duck hunt put a big dose of duck hunting fever in my blood stream. And well over fifty seasons later, I still ain't cured! Dad said it was an incurable disease. And of course, he was right again.

That was the only duck I shot during the season of '48, but after the seasons of '49 and '50, I had learned a lot more about the basics, lead, swing and follow through. Then, in the fall of '51, Dad informed me I had been invited to join Dad and a group of men who were planning a major opening week end duck hunt! And they were going to their favorite duck hunting spot. Devine Lake. It was like hearing Christmas was coming in October!

Duck season always opened on the first Saturday in October. Shooting hours for opening day were noon till sundown. By organizing and loading all our equipment Friday evening, we would be able to dive to Devine Lake, canoe to our campsite, set up camp and be in our blinds in time to be ready for the ducks by noon. Needless to say, I didn't sleep well Friday night!

Just getting to Devine Lake was an adventure! Nearly as exciting as the experience was once you got there! After turning our vehicles off a narrow town road, a two rut dirt trail twisted and turned through a forest of maple, birch and aspen for nearly a mile. The so called road ended abruptly at the crest of a steep hill that overlooked the valley which housed a trout stream named Mishonagon Creek. From here, all our gear and canoes had to be carried down the steep incline to the stream. Decoys, tents, blankets, food, cooking equipment, extra clothing, guns, shells, and etc. Going down the hill was a snap! Carrying it all back up again after the week end was over was another story!

Once the canoes and skiffs were loaded, they had to be pulled upstream through several hundred yards of a very shallow, rocky stretch of water. Then came the beaver dam! On a scale of one to ten this beaver dam was an eleven! Our overloaded craft had to be carefully lifted and dragged to the top of the dam, and then the occupants put their paddles to use. A quarter mile of easy paddling brought us to our destination. Devine Lake!

Devine Lake is a shallow, muddy, spring infested marsh containing a tremendous stand of wild rice. At least this was true fifty years ago. It was heaven for ducks. And also for duck hunters!

In the center of Devine Lake rests a large island, perhaps four or five acres in size. The island contained high, dry ground which was covered with lush stands of birch, balsam, and a scattering of assorted other hardwoods and pines. It was indeed a perfect location to camp.

The "gang" that invaded the island on opening week end of '51 consisted of five hunters and a black cocker spaniel. Uncle Bud, Charlie, Toby, Dad, me and Old Pat. By the time we erected our tents and organized the camp site, it was nearly eleven o'clock. Now it was off to our respective blinds, which the men had built the previous week end, and count the minutes as they ticked away till noon!

Toby usually hunted alone. He would paddle his low profile duck skiff to a handy muskrat house somewhere out in the thick stand of rice, and simply hide beside it. In the small area of open water around the 'rat house he would place a half dozen home made oversized black duck decoys. It was a deadly arrangement. Toby was without a doubt, the finest wing shot I have ever seen! When he pulled the trigger on his ancient square backed Belgium Browning 12 gauge, something fell from the sky.

Uncle Bud and Charlie teamed up and hunted from their blind on what Dad had dubbed, "No Ducks Point". At this location the rice was rather sparse and fewer ducks ventured there. But the lake bottom and the point contained solid, firm footing and decoys could easily be set and picked up without the aid of a canoe. Besides, both hunters had long ago learned that "just being there" was much more important than filling a limit. I hadn't learned that lesson yet.

Dad and me had our blind on the northeast shore, where a small spring crick lazily spilled it's water into Devine Lake. The meager flow was just enough to create a fairly large open area which allowed us to use a decoy spread which included several dozen fakes. Also, the bank was fairly firm with an abundance of tall grass and weeds, making concealment relatively easy. And Old Pat had some nice soft grass to rest on between retrieves.

But the members of our gang weren't the only duck hunters drawn to Devine Lake's lush rice beds. Generally there were four or five other blinds containing hunters scattered at various locations along it's marshy shores or situated within the thick rice itself. But there was more than enough room for all, and plenty of ducks to go around.

The vast majority of our local duck population a half century ago consisted primarily of black ducks. We referred to them as "black mallards". There were smaller numbers of common mallards, wood ducks, blue wing teal and ring necked ducks. But as the years passed, the common mallards soon outnumbered the black ducks. Being our continents most common duck, the common mallard has been steadily increasing in numbers and range, as it moves westward. Possibly someone suggested, "Go west young mallard, go west!"

Once noontime arrived it didn't take long for the harvest to begin. From uncounted pot holes, lakes and streams all of the north country the shooting began. And the ducks were on the move. Flocks numbering hundreds of birds would descend on Devine Lake. It was an awe inspiring spectacle that still remains vivid in my memory over a half century later!

Nearly fifteen thousand years ago, a glacier carved out a depression in the earth, which would eventually fill with water from the glacier as it melted and receded. Father Time added the rich muck from which the wild rice would flourish. Mother Nature surrounded this ancient amphitheater with trees to supply the dazzling array of fall colors, including reds, yellows, oranges, and greens. She then painted the roof a deep shade of blue and splashed in a few dab of white for a little contrast. Next, music was added via the air rushing over the cupped wings of incoming waterfowl. The finest Broadway production pales by comparison to having occupied a front row seat on Devine Lake on Opening Day. These were truly magic moments and cherished memories!

Devine Lake was good to us. No, make that wonderful to us. It presented us with a lifetime of sweet memories. These are memories of stories and talk around an evening campfire as the days harvest was cleaned. Gentle, but sound sleep in crisp fall air laced with the fragrance of balsam fir, moist soil, mushrooms and wood smoke. Being the rookie, I received expert instruction on subjects such as, respect for nature and all its varied creatures. A growing child needs companionship with adults to teach positive values by deed and example. And what better classroom to learn such valued information as the outdoors itself? And oh yes, Devine Lake also provided many, many duck dinners. I shot my first greenhead mallard there. And that milestone is truly a magic moment for any beginning duck hunter.

The Gang hunted together at Devine Lake on opening week end for four years. In the fall of '55 the junior member of the group drifted off to college and for reasons unknown to this author, the "Devine Lake Tradition" came to a close. But then again, we humans do and always will, live in a world of constant change. Old traditions give way to new ones.

I made my last trip to Devine Lake in October of 1959. Home from college for a week end duck hunt, I invited Uncle Shuck and Cousin Lee to share my final Devine Lake experience. I don't know how I knew this would be my final farewell to an old friend, but I knew.

It was late October. The vividly colored leaves of fall that had always been present on Opening Day were already faded, dry and curled on the forest floor. The white birches stood stark and naked among the darker oak, maple and pine. The stalks of wild rice, usually a rich yellow, splashed with tints of green, were likewise faded and drooping from several killing frosts. But the memories of the four Opening Week Ends I had spent there still burned bright in my memory.

We shot one lone hen mallard who was seduced into range by our dozen or so decoys. We paddled to the beaver dam and pulled our canoe over it one last time. As we descended Mishongon Creek we saw dozen of native brook trout spawning in the shallow gravel riffles. We carried our canoe and all our gear up the steep hill to our waiting vehicle for the last time.

We had completed an era.

# My Name Is "**Mister**" Sparks

Although the calendar didn't agree, summer was over! I knew summer had ended, at least for me and about four dozen other kids who lived in the township, because it was the day after Labor Day. A major obstacle eliminated our carefree days of summer. It was the first day of school and my first day in seventh grade! I had once again been sentenced to serve one hundred and sixty days in a penal institution known as the St. Germain State Graded School.

Oh, don't get me wrong about school. Actually school and me got along just fine. Except for English and Language classes. I never did care to study foreign language.

My classmates and I, all eight of us, made up the largest class in the St. Germain State Graded School, which imprisoned about fifty inmates in grades one through eight. The eight of us had been serving time together since September of 1943 when we had been found guilty of being six years old. For that crime we were incarcerated in the institution for eight years. We had already served six years of our sentence. But all in all, we had learned a lot of neat, new stuff.

Dad and Mom kept tellin' me how important gettin' an education was. I kept wondering what "an education" was, and when it was going to arrive. Well, on the memorable morning of my first day in seventh grade, a new form of education for all the kids in grades five through eight did arrive, shortly before eight a.m.!

The school I attended was built in 1941. The town's new school was a modern "two room" brick building, which replaced the ancient "one room" wooden model that had served the children of the community for many years. One room was called "The Little Room", although both classrooms were the same size, and housed the inmates in grades one through four. All subjects and all grades were taught by one teacher! The second classroom was called "The Upper Room". It contained prisoners from grades five through eight. Again, one teacher for all subjects and all grades. As I indicated earlier, we had gotten real progressive by 1941, doubling the size of the teaching staff!

At the time, our school district had but one bus. But is was a really big bus. It's seating capacity would accommodate twenty four kids, and up to thirty if the driver stuffed four kids to a seat. The bus was required to make "two runs" every morning and afternoon, in order to collect and discharge all fifty plus detainees that were scattered throughout the forty two square miles the comprised St. Germain School District Number One, et. all.

49

Due to the fact our single bus needed to make "two runs" each morning and each afternoon, the first load of students were unceremoniously dumped off in the schoolyard to "play" for nearly an hour before the second "bus run" brought the remainder of the inmates to the institution. In the afternoon, when school was dismissed at four p.m., the students who rode the bus home on the "second run" were left at school to "play" until the bus returned to pick them up and take them home. Of course, I use the word "play" in the broadest sense possible. Our play could more likely have been classed as a "semi-controlled riot".

During the first six years of my eight year sentence, the staff that guarded us, and attempted to pound some education into us, was make up entirely of female teachers. The school did have one male teacher/principal who taught fifth through eighth graders during my confinement in first and second grades. But Mr. Vandervort was at the end of his career and retired from teaching in the spring of 1945. Four years would pass before another male warden arrived in St. Germain.

First grade was kinda hectic. No less than three different teachers attempted pounding some knowledge into the heads of the twenty five or so first through fourth grader students that had been placed under their jurisdiction. Mrs. Polzin led off the first semester, but only lasted a couple of months.

Mrs. Swenson, who was picked up as a free agent, replaced Mrs. Polzin, and may have completed the school year if it hadn't been for Charles.

Charles was beginning his third year in fourth grade. I remember asking Dad and Mom why the guards were keeping Chuck in the Little Room so long. As we could tell by the thickness of his whiskers and the fact he was six feet two, he looked like he should have been close to collecting social security. Dad told me "Charles is different". Even as a first grader, I already knew that. The kids in the Upper Room said Chuck's bubble was about three quarters off plumb.

The end arrived for Mrs. Swenson sometime around late February. Charles had been "acting different" on the playground during noon hour, seeing how high in a tree he could toss first and second graders. He had been having one of his better days. For punishment, Mrs. Swenson put Chuck in solitary confinement under her desk! And then forgot he was there!

After her first afternoon class was over, Mrs. Swenson sat down at her desk to grade some papers. Seconds later, twenty five students levitated several feet above their desks as Mrs. Swenson emitted a blood curdling scream! Charles had seized the opportunity to attempt taking a bite out of his jailor's leg!

50

Meeting that night in emergency session, the Board of Education expelled Charles. Permanently! The second item on the agenda was to accept Mrs. Swenson's resignation. The students who occupied the Little Room completed the school term with a substitute, who's name escapes me.

The parade of teachers coming and going continued at a fairly steady and predictable pace. Mrs. Wolhaupt, pronounced "Wallhop", gave it her best try during the second year of my eight year sentence. (And you can probably guess what the students did with that name!)

Miss Sindicic became our matron during my third year of imprisonment. And of course we called her "Cindy's Sick" behind her back.

In my fourth year, Mrs. Sayner took her turn at bat. Actually Mrs. Sayner was one of the best teacher I ever had, but at the end of one year on the force, she called it quits.

The beginning of each school term was sorta like Christmas. You never know what you'll find when you opened a present. Only in the case of school, we never knew what we would find when we opened the classroom door.

And then, in September of 1947 the door to the Upper Room opened for me and my seven firth grade classmates. We had finally matured! And when we walked through the door, we found Miss Mildred Manley.

Miss Manley was young, slight of build, with a good crop of red hair and freckles. And a touch of Irish temper. She attempted to rule with an iron fist, which was the only way to handle twenty five convicts in one cell. Miss Manley lasted an unbelievable two years as our Upper Room teacher/principal! But like her five predecessors, the unmistakable signs of surrender began,...midway through her second year.

We had all seen those same signals before. The nervous twitch in the eye. The wringing of hands. The tearing of hair. (Both hers and ours) The gnashing of nails. The quiver in the voice. The tear stained cheeks. Stuttering. Weight loss. And an occasional shriek of madness. It was amazing how all of our teachers acted so much alike after a few months in the classroom.

Rumor had it that poor Miss Manley ended up in a padded white room at Sunnydale Acres for a few months after the end of the school term in May of 1949. But then again, it could have been just that, a rumor.

And then,...it was late August of '49, and seventh grade loomed near!

For several weeks prior to the beginning of my seventh year of incarceration in the St. Germain Grade School, the town was abuzz with rumors about the "new man teacher/principal the Board of Education had hired to,...as some adults put it,..."Straighten out that nest of hoodlums in the Upper Room."

All my buddies and classmates were wondering who those hoodlums were. After all, we had never seen any. All the kids were just like us. But the rumors did put a noticeable twitch in our stomachs. After all, none of us had ever seen a male teacher since Mr. Vandervort retired, let alone be guarded by one! The wait for school to begin during those final two weeks of carefree freedom were cloaked in mystery and suspense!

Now it's an established scientific fact that within every kid's body you can find three different kids. Sometimes more. First off, there's the kid who acts a certain way when they are with their friends and no parent or other adults are within sight or sound. Second, there is the kid who acts a certain way when they are at home or in the immediate reach of their parents. And thirdly, there is the kid who acts a certain way in school. The odd thing is, all three of these kids look the same, but they don't act the same. Sometimes it takes parents a while to discover this fact. And unfortunately, some parent never discover this fact, or won't admit it's true!

The day after Labor Day arrived! I happened to be one of the couple dozen inmates who were on the "first bus run", and had been dropped off at school to "play" until the bus returned from the "second bus run". As with all first days of a new school term the atmosphere was happy and fun filled, as the older inmates chased the younger ones around the schoolyard, filling their little hearts with fear. It was great, being a member of the second most macho class in school! And then,...the New Green Buick drove up to school and parked in one of the spaces reserved for officers of the institution.

It was a brand spankin' new 1950 Buick Special Two Door Sedan! The sparkling chrome wheels were offset by wide whitewall tires, and the sticker price was still glued to the rear side window. The playground riot ceased. We were certain the Buick had delivered our new teacher/principal. A knot of grinning kids gathered round the parked car.

The driver's door opened and out slizzered over six feet of masculine muscle and sinew. Young muscle and sinew! Dark brown wavy hair was combed immaculately and sat atop a finely chiseled face that slightly resembled that of Abraham Lincoln, without the beard. A perfectly knotted tie dangled in front of a freshly pressed white dress shirt, over which snuggly fit a bright red button up wool sweater. The crease in his tan dress pants was so sharp you could have whittled a stick with them. And I swear his pair of polished brown oxfords actually reflected the puffy white clouds that floated lazily in the dark blue September sky. Our new man teacher/principal was certainly a handsome specimen!

Showing no emotion, our new t/p slowly looked over the ring of faces starring up at him, most of which contained open mouths and slack jaws. And then a sixth grade boy, named Gary, made the first mistake of the morning.

52

Stepping forward, Gary acted as a self appointed greeter for the assembled inmates. Gary, a big smile on his innocent face proclaimed, "You must be Sparks."

With a motion quicker than a Hop-a-long Cassidy draw, a right hand shot out and grabbed a handful of Gary's shirt, just below his jaw. In one swift, powerful motion, Gary was jerked upward, his feet dangling two feet off the ground and his nose about six inches from that of our new warden!

"MY NAME IS MISTER SPARKS!", snarled Mr. Sparks. Then he opened his fist and Gary dropped to the ground in a tangled, quivering heap! Scowling a scowl more hideous than Dracula, the Wolf Man and Frankenstein combined, Mr. Sparks strode towards the school house door, as the throng before him parted like the waters of the Red Sea. As the door closed behind Mr. Sparks, a silence so silent, not known since the beginning of time, settled over the once noisy schoolyard. A new method of education had begun!

A very nervous and subdued group of fifth through eight graders slipped silently into the Upper Room a few seconds after the eight o'clock bell was rung by one of the fourth grade girls. A dark cloud of ominous foreboding hung like a gathering thunderhead as the Upper Room students eased quietly into their seats. It was so quiet the ticks of the classroom clock sounded like drumbeats. After what seemed like an eon, Mr. Sparks finally spoke.

"Good morning boys and girls. My name is MISTER Sparks. I introduced myself to some of you on the playground earlier this morning. His coal black eyes zeroed in on Gary, who was producing large beads of sweat on his forehead and trying unsuccessfully to swallow a lump the size of a softball. Students shifted uncomfortably in heir seats. The welcome continued.

For the next half hour we listened to Mr. Sparks, as he outlined his philosophy of teaching, what he expected from his students, and what his students could expect of him. Many of us had already seen first hand what we might expect from Mr. Sparks. Gary continued to look like a convicted felon on death row. Mr. Sparks finished his "First Day Of School Introductions" with a giant sized sermon about "respect", and "rules", and "responsibilities" and an assortment of other virtues that I suspected could only be found in saints or angels. Our future looked bleak indeed!

By nine a.m. our classes began. First came reading. The eight graders assembled around a long table in the middle of the "Upper Room", where most of our actual instruction took place. Each student took turns reading, as Mr. Sparks took notes and began to associate names with faces. Next came seventh grade reading class.

Mr. Sparks occupied a chair at the head of the table. Along its side to his left were seated the four seventh grade boys. Eugene, Yours Truly, Tom and Mike. To Mr. Spark's right were the four seventh grade girls. Dyann, Patty, Marion and Elaine. Mr. Sparks passed out the big, thick, orange "Prose and Poetry" reading books and began the lesson.

On command, we opened our books to the first story. It was a poem about some guy named Paul Revere and a horseback ride he took one night back in ancient times. Mr. Sparks pointed to the first boy on his left and asked for his name.

"Eugene" was the mumbled reply.

"You may begin reading, Eugene.", ordered Mr. Sparks.

Major mistake number two of the morning was fast in coming.. "I don't feel like reading.", mumbled Eugene.

Like a bolt of lighting, Mr. Spark's left hand swung in a short arc. The back of his hand caught Eugene flush in the face, sending him, his chair, and the orange Prose and Poetry Book sprawling on the classroom floor! In a blink of an eye, Mr. Sparks was on his feet, pulled Eugene to a standing position, replaced the chair and book, shoved Eugene back into his seat and commanded, "NOW READ!"

"Listen my children, and you shall hear, the midnight ride of Paul Revere." Between the waves of fear and disbelief that rippled through our minds and bodies, it was hard to believe that Eugene had learned to read so well and so quickly!

The days melted into weeks, and the weeks became months. The lessons continued. Some lessons were learned from our textbooks. Others by example, or deeds done. Other lessons were learned with a leather strap on the rear end, or a hard maple yard stick smacked on the back of your legs. For lesser crimes, one might simply be sentenced to washing blackboards for several days or weeks.

But a very strange thing happened to the upper grade students in the St. Germain School. We learned. We developed manners. We acquired respect for authority. We discovered rules and laws were necessary in order for society to function properly. And,...we learned those laws and rules needed to be obeyed! But the most amazing thing that happened was that not only had Mr. Sparks become our teacher/principal, he also became our friend!

My year in seventh grade finally evaporated in late May. My final year in grade school began early in September. Mr. Sparks was once again on hand to continue our education. But by his second year in command of the institution, very little time needed to be spent on discipline. An entire new atmosphere was present in our school! And it was an atmosphere of order, respect for each other and ourselves and our teacher. And oh yes, I almost forgot to mention school was fun!

Looking back on those two years I spent with Mr. Sparks, it is indeed easy to see they were a major turning point in my life. And a positive one I might add! Moving on to high school was easy, largely due to his presence in my life. And I suspect many of my classmates felt likewise. I hope so. It was Mr. Sparks who also helped me decide I not only wanted to be a fishing guide like Dad, but also a teacher.

And so, to Mr. Sparks and all the other teachers who gave so much of themselves for the betterment of their students, **THANK YOU!**

# Blizzard!

It was downright amazin' how much difference one year meant! I mean,...a year ago when I was thirteen, well,...I was pretty dumb. Why I even thought girls had no earthly use! But by the time fourteen rolled around, why,...I'd gained so many smarts I bean to think my brain couldn't possibly hold anymore! (It took a few more years before I began to re-evaluate my level of intelligence.)

Somewhere along the trail of life I ran across a tremendously witty and TRUE statement. It goes something like this. "When I was fourteen, I was ashamed of how stupid my parents were. When I was twenty one, I was amazed at how much those two had learned in just seven years."

Too bad it takes so long for some teenagers to realize just who the dummy really was. And even worse, some never figure it out.

Looking back, fourteen is the beginning of a really tough period for a kid to live through. Sometimes I seriously wonder how so many males actually survive the fourteen through the eighteen year era. (And I've wondered about some who still act like fourteen year olds at thirty five!) Having now lived well into my sixth decade of life here on earth, I am convinced most teen age males make it into their twenties mostly on luck.

Well, enough adult editorializing. Back to my adventure.

Besides increasing my total knowledge by several thousand percent in less than one year, other noticeable changes in my maturity occurred. As Dad Anderson put it, "The sap was rapidly rising." (If teen age boys were like maple trees, their parent could "tap the sap" each spring and increase their offspring's chances of survival.)

I still suspected some of the Greek Philosophers and men like Edison and Watt, and Bell perhaps were a tad smarter than myself, but generally, my total knowledge and nearly supernatural common sense put me in the upper one percent on the list of smartest humans on the planet. There was no doubt! But an event occurred during the deer season of 1951 that would drop my name much lower on the list.

It was Sunday afternoon, the second day of Wisconsin's 1951 deer season. All eighteen of the visiting hunters, who had filled the bunks in the Anderson-Jorgensen Hunting Camp, had already departed with all their tags filled. As Dad had predicted, it had been a slaughter! The Conservation Department, in a continuing effort to reduce a deer herd who's population was out of control, had made all deer legal targets. The amount of shooting on opening day rivaled that of the Normandy Invasion! The "meat pole" had never supported so many dead deer.

But Dad and I had opted to not fill our tags so quickly. We had helped other hunters in our camp to get some venison, but our tags remained unfilled. With still nearly a week to hunt, why ruin you deer season by filling your tag with a doe on opening day? We hadn't.

It was shortly after lunch when Dad and I ambled west, down our driveway and crossed County Highway C. Our destination was "The Big Ravine", an ancient dried up river valley that had been carved out thousands of years earlier when the last great continental glacier melted. The Big Ravine was, at the time, an open expanse of grasslands about two hundred yards wide, running north and south. The east and west ridges, which overlooked the ravine, were covered with second growth jack pine and aspen. Although we called aspen "popple". Dozens of major deer runways crossed the ravine. It was one of our gang's favorite deer hunting areas! And on this afternoon it belonged to just Dad and me!

Within twenty minutes, we had eased to the top of the ravine's eastern ridge. Looking north and south, as far as we could see, was nothing but a snow carpeted landscape. Not one other "redcoat" could be seen! Dad and I had our pick of any location we wished to choose for our afternoon hunt. I was given first choice.

"Well", Dad whispered, "Which way are you goin'?"

"North", I unhesitatingly whispered back.

"O.K.", Dad agreed. "I'll head south a few hundred yards and find a good looking runway to watch. I'll meet you back by our mailbox at the end of our driveway after shooting hours."

I nodded by head in agreement and grinned to let Dad know I fully understood his directive.

Dad smiled back in return, gave me one of his best winks, and added, "Good Luck Buckshot. Shoot a big one!"

I answered with a "thumbs up", and headed north. I knew exactly which runway I would watch. The same one where Dad bagged an eight pointer and a six pointer just minutes apart back in '46. I mean, being able to watch that runway, how could I miss?

As I slowly and carefully made my way northward, I marveled at how rapidly I had mastered the art of woods-man-ship. Why, I could slip through the forest with hardly a sound! I had wandered throughout this vast wilderness for the past several years. I knew every tree and blade of grass by its first name! I could probably find my way back home blindfolded! In the dark yet! I hadn't considered finding my way home in a blizzard.

Gradually, ever so slowly, the hazy overcast sky had thickened. The gentle southwest breeze had gradually swung to the northeast. Funny, but the "Master of Woods-man-ship" had not noticed. Nor did he hardly notice nor pay any attention to the first scattered snowflakes that began floating earthward about two p.m.

By three p.m. the wind had picked up considerably, along with the falling snow. In fact, snow was now falling in massive sheets, driven nearly horizontally by a howling northeast wind! Piles of wet, sticky snow began to accumulate on my shoulders and hat. The branches of the drooping jack pine, under which I was standing, whipped back and forth with the force of the ever intensifying wind.

"What a luck break!", I thought. "Just the kind of weather change that will make deer look for a sheltered spot to ride out a snow storm. A big old buck will be sure to cross the ravine on this runway any minute!" Such are the dreams of youth.

Darkness descended quickly and early, due to the thickening clouds, as the nor'easter intensified. Wind gusts shook my jack pine shelter like a dog shaking a rag doll! Snowflakes, driven by a brutally gusting wind, stung my bare face like driven sand. Suddenly, I felt the need to head towards home and meet Dad at our mailbox. The sudden descent of near darkness sent the first pang of panic through my insides! It was time to leave. It was time to meet Dad!

I navigated the first hundred yards at a fairly modest pace. After all, I knew my way back to our designated meeting spot. But then, something looked wrong! In the rapidly deepening gloom, nothing looked familiar! Trees I knew by their first names had become strangers! My earlier pang of panic increased in size to a knot of panic! My pace doubled!

Driving snow pelted my face and eyes, making my eyes water. The sickening lump in my stomach slid quickly to my throat. Tears joined the snow driven water streaming from my eyes! I was lost!

As I stumbled onward, not knowing where I was nor where I was headed, my short life began to pass before my watering eyes. I plunged ahead through the darkening forest as whirlwinds of wind driven snow swirled around my trembling body. Never, since my flight through the fog shrouded Minnow Pond Swamp five years ago with Cousin Lee, had I experienced such fear. I tried to vomit, but nothing came up. I staggered on!

As I wandered aimlessly through the rapidly deepening snow, I began to recall stories I had listened to in the deer hunting shack. Stories about hunters lost in blizzards. Bodies that weren't found till spring! Hunters who slowly froze to death, after their last ounce of strength hand been squeezed from their chilled bodies! Some stories had included the comforting information that freezing to death wasn't such a terrible way to die. You just kinda went to sleep and never woke up! How did they know that? Dead men don't talk! I tried to cry harder, but my tear ducts had already been drained dry.

Then suddenly I stopped! What was that I spied in the snow crossing my path? I bent lower to examine the tracks which had caught my attention. THEY WERE BOOT TRACKS! Someone else was near! All I had to do was follow these tracks and at least I'd have a companion when we froze to death! I rushed onward, following those wonderful boot print in the deepening snow!

But then another deer hunting shack story leaped into my memory! The story about the dumb city slicker who walked in circles, following his own footprints. And all the time wondering who all those other people were walking in front of him. Perhaps these prints were my own. Maybe my unknowing wanderings was causing me to travel in circles! Once again the knot of fear returned!

I kneeled down to more closely inspect the footprints I had been following. They were definitely larger than those made my by feet and the tread imprint seemed to be different. I wasn't following myself! I rushed forward once again.

Unexpectedly, I burst from the evil, dark forest into what I first thought was an opening in the forest. My first suspicion was that I was once again on the ridge overlooking the Big Ravine. But no! I was standing on the edge of a road! It must be Highway C! Now I knew where I was. Hey! There's someone standing over yonder by a mail box! My entire body relaxed. It was Dad!

In a split second all the pieces of the puzzle fell into place. The boot tracks I had been following had been his! What a stoke of woods-man-ship on my part. Dad spoke.

"Well Buckshot, did you see anything?"

Trying to control my erratic breathing, I answered, "Nope. Didn't see a thing. Stayed on my stand right up to nearly full dark too. Thought for sure an old buck would come my way, headin' for cover. But no luck." (I hoped the pitch of my voice hadn't given away my secret.)

"Same here", Dad replied, "Nothin' crossed by me either. Let's head for home and see what yer mom's cooked for supper."

Side by side we walked the final quarter mile to our home. But it was many years later before I leveled with Dad as to what had REALLY happened to me after I left my stand during that nor'easter. And the "confession" made me feel good.

As I lay in bed later that night, I began to suspect my acquired level of woods-man-ship might just need a tad more honing before I received my Master's Degree. Fifty plus years later I'm still honing!

# Brule Barrens Sharptails, (and more!)

Dad and Mom Anderson had a neat plan when they raised me. At least I think it was a plan. It always seemed they would promise me something I really wanted badly, IF,...I'd do my chores, get good grades in school, or some other sort of prearranged suggestion.

Well, whether or not it was a plan or not a plan, the system worked well. At least as far as I was concerned. I sure got to do a lot of neat things I wanted to do or try to do. And I don't ever remember Dad or Mom not following through with their promises, IF,...I followed through with what I was supposed to accomplish first. I think our arrangement worked out well for all three of us.

As I recall, it was sometime during the late summer of '52 when I got the "Sharptail Promise". I'd been cuttin' popple pulpwood most of the summer to make a few dollars, which hopefully would tide me through my sophomore year in high school. It was the second summer I had been imitating being a logger. The previous summer of '51 had been my rookie year loggin' off some of the mature aspen trees which covered much of the woods Dad and Mom owned.

Dad challenged me by giving me a single blade ax and his Swede saw, and turned me loose on the aspen, which we called popple. I worked my buns off, fighting mosquitoes, black flies, and blackberry briars, to make a little spendin' money. I'll never forget the amount I had for profit, after I paid to rent a horse so Dad could skid out my logs, and then pay for the truck that hauled my harvest to the mill. A cool $200.50! Well, during the summer of '52, after banking all that experience from my first lumbering season, I pocketed $450.00! And I put to rest for all time the former glorious idea I once had of becoming a lumberjack!

In between cutting pulpwood, Dad put me to work helpin' him guide fishermen. I really didn't feel rowin' fishermen around some lake so they could catch a few fish was work. But then again pullin' on a pair of six and a half foot white spruce oars for six or seven hours a day did make me sleep real good. But as long as I could do a little fishin' in between the pullin', it didn't seem like work. At least not work like cutin' and peelin' and stackin' popple pulpwood! I knew right then and there I was going to be a real guide, someday. Just like Dad! I suppose that was part of his plan too.

Well anyway, the requirement involving the "Sharptail Promise" required me to do good in school so I'd be eligible to go with Dad and Uncle Emil, plus several more of Dad's buddies, on a hunt for shaprtail grouse up north in the Brule Barrens. Whatever those Brule Barrens were.

There were two major incentives for my consideration in this promise. One: I'd never been on a hunt for just sharptail grouse before. I had shot a couple by "accident" once, thinking they were ruffed grouse. And two: I'd get to skip school for two days! It was hard to decide which incentive thrilled me most. But they sure enough were two dandies!

Back when I was a kid, summers seemed to last forever. (Now as I slide into my mid sixties, summers slip by in a couple blinks of an eye!) Well, the summer of '52 crept along, and then school slowed the creep to a snail's crawl, when classes began right after Labor Day. Me and high school was gettin' along real good, except for that foreign language class, called English. I kept wishin' they'd just replace English with a new course called "American", but it was not to be.

September doddled along until the last week end, and then Dad, me, and Old Pat got in a week end of hunting our local ruffed grouse, which we called "partridges". And right after that it was October!

I sure wish whoever invented the calendar would have put about two hundred days in October. That would have been wise, as duck, grouse and woodcock seasons would have lasted a lot longer. But at least we got thirty one days out of the deal. I often wondered why February got short changed.

During the second week of October the big day finally arrived. Eight of us piled into two cars and headed north up U.S. 51, and then swung west on U.S. 2 towards those Brule Barrens. The trip took about three hours. We rented a couple of small cabins in the little hamlet of Brule, Wisconsin and made our plans for the opening day of sharptail season. There was no doubt I was the most excited hunter in the group!

And it was quite a diverse group Dad had assembled. The list included Dad's oldest brother, Uncle Emil, three of Dad's buddies, Charlie, Toby and Bill, plus Dad, me, Old Pat and Toby's Springer Spaniel, Freckles.

Uncle Emil was really old. He was in his early sixties. He had shot lots of sharptails when he was young, around the Anderson farm in Mountain, Wisconsin. Later, Uncle Emil moved west to Idaho and continued to work in the logging industry, following the footsteps of Grandpa Anderson. Uncle Emil happened to come back to Wisconsin for a visit, just in time to get invited to the Brule Barrens. While he was staying at our house, I showed him my piles of pulpwood. Uncle Emil was pretty impressed. At least he told me he was.

Like me, Charlie was on his first sharptail hunt. Charlie make a couple of comments that he hoped this hunt would turn out better than his first trout fishin' trip with Dad and me on the Pine. Charlie had reluctantly volunteered to use his Buick on this outing too. He all too well remembered the pounding his then new Buick had taken on that trout fishing expedition back in June of '50. Dad assured Charlie that his car couldn't get damaged on this trip, because we'd only be drivin' on improved roads. Dad also guaranteed nothin' could possibly hurt Charlie's baby on this trip. The trouble with guarantees is that they often don't cover all types of disasters.

Toby was without a doubt the best wing shot I ever knew. He was even a little better than Dad. Toby hunted with an old Belgium Browning square back 12 gauge, and when he cut loose at ducks, grouse, geese, or whatever, they dropped! He was a magician with a scattergun.

Bill had a somewhat limited experience with hunting in general, but he seemed to carry himself like a guy who would do o.k. We'd find out in the morning.

Dad had hunted the Brule Barrens several times in previous years, and knew the lay of the land. He'd be our guide. Dad came by that trait naturally. I'd just tag along and do what I was told to do. But I was happy and excited to have been included in the hunt and was being treated like "one of the guys". We were really doing what much later became known as "male bonding", but we didn't have the slightest hint we were so far ahead of the times.

Shortly after sunup the following morning, our guide led five eager hunters to the edge of the Brule Barrens. The Barrens consisted of thousands of acres of grasslands, interspersed with groves of small trees and brushy thickets. Although somewhat similar in appearance, ruffed grouse and sharptail grouse inhabit very different habitat. While the ruffies long for dense cover, the sharpies prefer the open grasslands and scattered thickets. And where we were going to hunt was certainly prime sharptail country!

Our plan of attack was fairly simple. Starting at the edge of a likely looking field, the six of us would spread out in a long line, about thirty yards apart, and slowly walk the length of the field. Then we'd swing left or right, line up again and repeat the sequence. And while we were walkin', our two dogs did a lot of runnin', findin' those sharptails and makin' 'um fly for us to bang away at. When the entire field had been searched, we'd get in the cars and drive to another field.

As with most simple plans, it worked great! At least for those gunners who occupied the center and inside portions of the line. It didn't take long for the rookies to discover the feeding shaptails were usually out toward the center of the fields and not close to the edge of the trees and thickets. So the hunter who was assigned the outside of the line, nearest the edge of the field, didn't get in on much of the shooting. I was assigned the outside of the line. I started to feel I might as well had stayed home and went to school. Well, not really.

The day dragged on. Field after field was combed and the adults were getting all kinds of shooting at those flushing sharpies. The pile of bagged birds in the trunks of our cars grew higher and higher. Oh, I did take a few long shots at departing birds when my companions missed now and then, although my shots were shots of desperation and despair.

It was about 4:30 in the afternoon when we arrived at what would be our last field of the day. It was smaller than most of the fields we had hunted and trudged around. Dad figured we could make one quick sweep around the field and be back at the cars in a half hour or less. Uncle Emil was pooped out and opted to stay in Charlie's car, curl up in the back seat and take a nap. The remainded of our group lined up, loaded our shotguns and headed out.

The small field appeared to hold no additional sharptails. The ragged line of hunters was nearing the completion of our circle around the field. The hunters who occupied the inside and center of the line were nearing the cars, and I could hear the actions of their shotguns clicking as they unloaded their weapons. Being the outside of the line person again, I still had a little over a hundred yard to cover before I reached the vehicles. And then, right smack dab in front of me, Old Pat hit a hot scent!

Luck seemed to be on my side for a change, as none of the other hunters saw the drama that was unfolding. And the kid who hadn't shot a single bird all day was not about to call their attention to the situation! This would be my last chance to prevent being "skunked" on opening day!

Old Pat's stub tail was rotating a million miles an hour, and his sniffing and snuffing was making the tall dead grass wiggle. I knew the sharptail would soon take wing, as we were getting close to the road on which the cars were parked.

Old Pat finally came to a stop, took a look over his shoulder at me to make sure I was ready, and then he made a sudden pounce into a tangled clump of tall grass. The startled sharptail gave out a series of clucks as it took wing, angling to my left and heading for the next field on the far side of the road. My entire world was centered on that departing bird as my little 20 gauge side by side slid crisply to my shoulder. I swing the bead swiftly past its head and pulled the front trigger.

Trailing a small puff of brown feathers, the bird crashed to the grass covered field. Old Pat was on it before the lifeless body stopped rolling. The memory of my earlier fruitless hunt evaporated like a morning fog.

None of the other hunters had witnessed my moment of triumph. However, at the sound of my shot, all heads spun in my direction just in time to see Old Pat delivering the goods to the marksman who had bagged the bird. Wasn't I the hero now! My fame turned out to be short lived.

As I was bending down to take my prize from Old Pat, I heard two sounds in rapid succession. One: The slamming of a car door. And two: Uncle Emil yelling, "WHO FIRED THAT SHOT?"

I proudly held up my quarry and responded, "ME!"

Uncle Emil looked unimpressed and upset. His next remark told me why.

"YOUR LOAD OF FINE SHOT HIT CHARLIE'S BUICK!"

If I'd had a shovel, I'd have dug a hole and crawled in. I doubt if I was ever more embarrassed in my life. And beside that, I was instantly scared! I was sure I'd be executed, or worse!

Charlie's response did little to suggest my worst fears were not well founded. "BUCKSHOT SHOT MY CAR?" I knew what color Charlie's face would be. And my backside would probably be the same color when Dad got done with me. My stomach felt like wiggling Jello.

I removed the unfired shell from my shotgun and as slowly as possible walked to the angry mob which was huddled around Charlie's Buick assessing the damage. I wondered how long I'd need to cut pulpwood so I could buy Charlie a new Buick.

Dad spoke. "Didn't you see Charlie's car was in your line of fire before you pulled the trigger? Haven't I told you a million times to look beyond your target BEFORE you shoot? I've never seen you do something like this before. You aught to be ashamed of yourself! Look what you did to Charlie's fender."

I looked. The major portion of Charlie's left rear fender contained dozens of pock marks from the portion of my load of number six shot that had missed the sharptail. I was impressed at how nice the pattern was, even at over seventy yards. The Buick looked like it had chicken pox.

I looked at Charlie and managed to squeak out a heartfelt apology. I told him I would pay to have the fender repainted and added I'd never do such a stupid thing again. And I've kept that second promise for over a half century.

I figured Dad would impound my shotgun, making it impossible for me to make another blunder like the one at hand, but he didn't. In fact, the possibility of a death sentence seemed to be fading. I got a major lecture about how my carelessness could really have hurt Uncle Emil if he had been standing by the car when I shot. Dad also gave me a quick refresher course on gun safety, which I already knew by heart. He ended his sermon with, "And if you ever come close to doing something this stupid again, your gun will be retired. PERMANENTLY!"

.The trial was over and the sentence had been rendered. A couple of the adults added a reminder that everyone makes mistakes, but only the wise learn from them. They said they hoped I had learned something by this one. And I had. My scolding was a small price to pay for a very large error.

We hunted two more days in those wonderful Brule Barrens and I was even given the opportunity to hunt the middle of the line. I got my share of shooting and a few more birds. It was a great experience. Other than shooting Charlie's Buick. And although I offered several times, Charlie didn't make me pay to have his fender repainted.

I was fortunate to be able to hunt the Barrens two additional times, once in '54 and again in '55. Dad's group did well in '54, but then the Department of Natural Resources planted nearly all the open field area with pine seedlings. By October of '55 the large flocks of sharptails were in rapid decline, and in several years had all but vanished. Their habitat had been ruined, and the Sharptails of the Brule Barrens were no more! I never could understand why jack pine trees were more important than a home for sharptails. So much for "progress".

I shot my last sharptail in '55 on my last hunt in the Barrens. Since then I've done lots of hunting for lots of other game in lots of different places. But hunting those sharptails was one of my most memorable experiences. In recent years, the Department of Natural Resources has begun re-establishing sharptail habitat in Wisconsin. If they hadn't ruined it back in the 50's, it would have saved them a lot of extra work. To say nothing of saving the sharptails! But at least the Department's efforts need to be applauded.

In the fall of 1998 I traveled to the Colorado Rockies and shot my first elk. He was a magnificent 5 x 5 bull that hit the scales at slightly over seven hundred and fifty pounds. But that was still about a ton smaller than the Buick I bagged back in 1952!

# The Slaying Of "Slewfoot"

The north woods was in the icy grip of late December. The snow stood waist deep and the daytime temperatures never seemed to be able to struggle out of the single digits. Daylight lasted but a scant nine hours, as the sun strained in vane to climb beyond the crowns of the ancient red pines that rimmed The Lake. The winter season, although in it's infancy, was passing with the speed of a frozen snail. It was a wonderful time to be a boy!

\*\*\*\*\*\*\*\*\*\*\*\*\*\*\*\*\*\*\*\*\*\*\*\*\*\*\*\*\*\*\*\*\*\*\*\*\*\*\*\*\*\*\*\*\*\*\*\*\*\*\*\*\*\*\*\*\*\*\*\*\*\*\*\*
\*\*\*\*\*\*

Never let it be said that winters are, or ever were, a time with "nothing to do" or "boring". Dad told me the only people who get bored are boring people. And I don't have to remind you that Dad was right again. Winter holds a special magic for kids of all ages who can discover beauty and adventure during the season of virgin white. And so it was with me, the anticipation of winter weekends made the school week an endurable intermission.

The Stoeckmann's purchased the old Noble homestead and moved in to become year around residents during the summer of 1950. There were two boys in the Stoeckmann household, Bob, four years my senior and Roger, a year older than myself. We quickly became good friends.

Roger and I had exactly the same burning desire, when it came to doing anything that involved the out of doors. It mattered not if the activity was fishing, or hunting, or trapping, or building tree houses, or just roaming around exploring some new niche of nature. For the first time in my life I had a friend who lived within a reasonable distance from the Anderson homestead.

The trip by snowshoe, from where the Andersons lived to the Stoeckmann residence, took about fifteen minutes. Roger was just getting his boots on when I pounded the snow from mine and entered the Stoeckmann's cozy kitchen. Mr. & Mrs. Stoeckmann were still eating breakfast, but took time to ask how Dad and Mom were, and wish Roger and I a safe and successful day in the out of doors. Within minutes Roger and I, along with Old Pat, were on our way towards Little Duck Lake Swamp, where within its tangled interior were homes for many snowshoe hares.

Despite the snow depth, the half mile trek to Little Duck Lake Swamp was an easy walk. Past outings to this destination had packed a cement hard snowshoe trail that allowed us to cover the distance in less than fifteen minutes. Having fifteen year old legs also helped a great deal! Old Pat, with his long curly earls a floppin' raced ahead, fully aware of what lay in store for this trio of hunters. He, like his human companions, had made this trip many times.

Reaching the northwestern edge of our targeted hunting location, our plan was quickly rehearsed. Roger would continue east along the swamp's border, then swing south into the bowels of it's interior, and take up a position where several major snowshoe hare runways intersected. Here, he and his single shot 16 gauge shotgun would attempt to ambush any snowshoes traveling along their highways. Old Pat and I would march south and west, following the swamp's edge for another quarter mile. Then we would plunge into the tangle of black spruce trees and attempt to move some hiding hares form their havens towards the watchful eyes of our companion. It was a simple plan we had used successfully many times.

Ten minutes later I pushed the button to begin the hunt. On command, Old Pat plunged into the deep snow and plowed his way toward the swamp's interior. It was here he would find the criss cross pattern of hare runways which were packed nearly as solidly as our own snowshoe paths. Old Pat knew his business!

Hardly ten minutes elapsed before the roar of Roger's 16 gauge violated the stillness of the winter morning. I suspected a meal of fresh snowshoe hare had just been secured. A few minutes later the scenario was repeated. The meal would now probably provide a second helping.

Reaching Roger's location, his beaming face confirmed my suspicions. Two snow-white young hares rested on the snow by his feet. We tied them to his belt and began phase two of our planned activity. Another fifteen minute hike over Hunter's Ridge would place us at our next destination, Franke's Swamp.

As our snowshoes crunched, compacting the newly fallen snow adding yet another layer to our familiar path, we chatted about past outings, took in the beauty that surrounded us, and tried to guess what new adventures lay before us. As I said earlier, it was a wonderful time to be a boy!

Roger, who was in the lead, suddenly stopped and pointed to a fresh track in the fluffy snow. There, on one of the well traveled snowshoe hare trails that crossed the high ground between the two swamps, was the largest hare track either of us had ever seen! The imprints of the hare's hind feet were one third longer than any other rabbit track we had ever observed. And the two of us had viewed hundreds, if not thousands!

We looked at each other with wide, unbelieving eyes. The hare that had made these tracks was now hiding somewhere in the sixty plus acres of Franke's Swamp! We JUST had to get him! We plunged onward with renewed energy and magnified anticipation!

During the remainder of our hunt that day we crossed the tracks of what we guessed must be a "giant rabbit" several more times. And although we did bag several more snowshoes, "big foot" was not included in our total. But what the heck, we had all winter ahead of us, and Old Pat was sure to flush him by one of our waiting guns sooner or later.

But it was not to be. We put our shotguns away for the season in late February and the elusive "big foot" was still running free. But in the meantime, we had somehow christened our invisible quarry with a new name. "Slewfoot".

\*\*\*\*\*\*\*\*\*\*\*\*\*\*\*\*\*\*\*\*\*\*\*\*\*\*\*\*\*\*\*\*\*\*\*\*\*\*\*\*\*\*\*\*\*\*\*\*\*\*\*\*\*\*\*\*\*\*\*
\*\*\*\*\*\*

Ten months passed. The landscape of Northern Wisconsin was once again blanketed beneath a deep mantle of virgin white. Gone were the carefree days of summer, which had given Roger and I so many memories of fishing, swimming, playing softball, socializing with the teen age female tourists, and a host of other memorable summer activities. Gone were the breathtakingly beautiful days of fall, which had found Roger and I hunting grouse, ducks and deer. Now began three months of once more traveling about our winter wonderland on snowshoes, chasing the "gray ghosts of the thickets". It was a wonderful time to be a boy!

\*\*\*\*\*\*\*\*\*\*\*\*\*\*\*\*\*\*\*\*\*\*\*\*\*\*\*\*\*\*\*\*\*\*\*\*\*\*\*\*\*\*\*\*\*\*\*\*\*\*\*\*\*\*\*\*\*\*\*
\*\*\*\*\*\*

Life often supplies one with an unexpected surprise, and on our very first snowshoe hare outing in mid December, Roger and I received a dandy! Once again we crossed the tracks of Slewfoot! Our unseen adversary had survived the seasons and was once again challenging our skill as hunters. Slewfoot had certainly out foxed us the winter past, but now he was dealing with two determined woodsmen who had, (at least in our minds) matured greatly during the past year. Time would tell.

Weekend after weekend flitted by, and hunt as hard as we could, Old Slewfoot still remained unseen. Perhaps we were chasing a real ghost! Maybe Slewfoot was simply the soul of all the showshoes we had bagged over the past several winters. Possibly Slewfoot had been sent here by some higher power to wreck havoc on our egos! And then it was once again late February, and we were nearing the end of our season to hunt hares.

Roger and I had just emerged from the depths of Franke's Swamp, after a long and difficult day of chasing gray ghosts. Light snow had begun drifting down from a lead-lined sky shortly after noon, and as the afternoon wore on had developed into a full-blown snow storm. We decided to call it quits for the day and were heading homeward. Old Pat limped along behind us on our well packed trail, his leg "feathers" encrusted with ice balls, and panting our a message of near exhaustion.

Before us rose a minor ridge that separated Franke's Swamp from The Lake. Beyond the crest of the ridge were two tiny swamps, infested with small black spruce trees, nestled at the eastern edge of The Lake. Once past these two swamps, Roger and I would part company. He would strike out southwestward across The Lake towards his home and I would take a northwesterly route to mine. But as sometimes happens, Fate dealt us a new card.

At the crest of the ridge our snowshoe path intersected a major hare runway that connected the two tiny swamps at the edge of The Lake with Franke's Swamp. The runway was normally only used by hares during nighttime hours. But etched in the freshly fallen snow was the unmistakable imprint of Slewfoot! For whatever reason our mystery rabbit had decided to vacate the vast interior of Franke's Swamp and head for the tiny swamps that lay before us! We couldn't believe our luck at this unexpected turn of events!

It appeared that Slewfoot had put himself in peril. If indeed his fresh track entered the southernmost of the two small swamps, and had not continued over the narrow spit of high ground that separated it from the northernmost swamp,...well, Old Slewfoot would be boxed in. We would have him cornered! At last he would be ours! But then again, hadn't we shared similar thoughts many times over the past two winters?

Following Slewfoot's fresh trail another hundred yards we discovered he had indeed entered the southernmost swamp. Roger volunteered to stop at the point where the runway Slewfoot had used entered the swamp. I would ease onward to the narrow finger of high ground that separated the two small swamps. We would still be in eye contact with each other when I checked the single runway that ran between the two tiny swamps. If Slewfoot had not crossed, I would signal Roger to plunge into Slewfoot's hiding haunt and flush him in my direction!

It took less than two minutes for me to reach my destination. A quick examination of the runway which connected the two swamps indicated that nothing had crossed since the snow had begun several hours earlier. Slewfoot WAS in the first swamp!

At a wave of my hand, Roger eased into the swamp and out of sight. Old Pat lay at my side, still panting. My arms and legs began trembling a bit, knowing Roger would follow Slewfoot's tracks and push him my way. The runway I was guarding was his only exit.

Several minutes passed. The snowfall continued to intensify and gusts of raw wind drove stinging snowflakes onto my face and into my watering eyes. And then it happened!

A speeding blur of gray came bounding out of the tiny swamp, heading pell mell towards the entrance to the second swamp. The safety on my little double barreled 20 gauge snapped off and the stock settled crisply on my shoulder. I swung the front bead ahead of Slewfoot and pulled the trigger. The soft snow exploded just behind the fleeing form of the mystery rabbit Roger and I had been searching for during the past two winters. I had missed! I lengthened my lead by two feet and touched off the second barrel. Slewfoot and one ounce of number six shot met each other just as he was about to vanish into the second swamp.

My shots rejuvenated Old Pat and he sprang into action. The Old Professional had the subject of our quest at my feet in a matter of seconds. The many long hours of searching had ended. We had won! At last, Slewfoot was ours!

Roger emerged from the snow-shrouded swamp, looking much like Frosty the Snowman. "Did ya get 'im?" he asked, his voice filled with doubt. I held up our trophy and grinned. And then Roger had to listen to "The Story".

Taking our first good look at Slewfoot resulted in yet another unexpected surprise. What we thought would be a giant bunny, judging from the size of his tracks, turned out to be a skinny, puny midget. "Strange", we thought. But then we surmised that possibly this hare had used all his youthful energy to just grow big feet. It was time to head home.

After cleaning my game and depositing the tasty meat in the kitchen sink for Mom to prepare, I had to tell and retell Dad and Uncle Bud all about how Roger and I spent the better part of two winters chasing a gray ghost we had named "Slewfoot". They patiently listened, but didn't seem to get very excited.

Later that night, as I lay in my bed replaying the day's events in my mind, and remembering how hard Roger and I had hunted in order to kill Slewfoot, I received another surprise. I actually felt a tinge of sadness. I then realized, for the first time in my life, the planning and effort expended to gain something of perceived value is often more rewarding and challenging than actually achieving your goal. Dad, Mom and Uncle Bud had suggested this concept to me many times, but I had never understood what they were actually trying to tell me. But on this night, nestled in my warm bed, I understood!

Maybe, just maybe, I had matured a bit in the past year!

# June 30th, 1953; "A Day That Lives In Infamy!"

Nineteen fifty three was a great year! Except for June thirtieth. And even then, the thirtieth was only terrible for a few hours. But those few terrible hours supplied my brain with some terrifying images that are still vividly recalled in my memory.

Nineteen fifty three! WOW! A lot of wonderful things happened in my life during that year. But, as I indicated earlier, a bit of real bad stuff happened too. First some of the good stuff.

In February of that wonderful '53, I turned sixteen. I don't know how sweet I was at sixteen, but all that stuff about "sweet sweet sixteen and never been kissed" sure wasn't true anymore.

By the end of March I had my drivers license. Even though getting a drivers license is a major event in most persons lives, Dad and Mom rarely let me drive the family car unless they were passengers. Except on Prom Night, when I got to use our big, long, black, '49 Buick to haul my date to the prom and back. But that's another story. And another pretty good memory!

With that driver's license came my first guide license. Oh, I'd been following Dad around on the lakes a few times during the past two summers, trying unsuccessfully to get the hang of what guides are supposed to do. Mainly find some fish for their clients to catch. But, as I found out much later, learning the "tricks of the trade" didn't happen overnight. Nor even in a few years. But with that first drivers license came the ability for me to be able to strike out on my own, and start the long learning process. By Opening Day in May of '53 I was ready! A second generation of fishing guides, with the last name of Anderson, was turned loose on the lakes and streams of Northern Wisconsin! And another of my many youthful dreams had come true!

Since 1949, when Mom and Dad had finally finished building "The Lodge" at our resort and started serving meals as well as lodging, a large group of anglers from Wausau, Wisconsin had been housed, fed and guided at Kasomo Lodge. A gentleman by the name of Mr. Duetch, whom my Dad had been guiding for many years, was the leader of our "Opening Weekend" clients. As usual, Mr. Duetch instructed Dad to hire enough guides to accommodate the thirteen men who would be staying at our resort. And in 1953 I would be one of those who were hired. Besides Dad and myself, five additional guides were needed to serve the "Duetch Gang".

There was Don Freund, a massive six foot four inch giant, with a permanent grin on his friendly face, who made pulling on the oars look like fun and child's play. A seasoned veteran of many seasons, "Big Don" was a favorite of any and all who partook of his services.

Toby Andersen, one of Dad's best pals, had only been guiding for a few seasons, but could best be described as "an outdoorsman's outdoorsrman". Everything in the line of fishin' huntin' or trappin' just seemed to come naturally to Toby. And everybody liked Toby!

"Red" Yeager, worked at any number of part time jobs and did a fair amount of guiding during the summer months. A quiet, laid back likeable chap, he also played one heck of a game at shortstop for the men's softball team. Had Red gotten a chance to attend college, there is little doubt in my mind that he may have landed a job in the Major Leagues. He was that good!

Dick Merrill owned a small resort and bar on Lost Lake and filled in as a guide for many large groups of visiting anglers. Good natured and friendly, he certainly would fit in well with this team of professionals. And besides, Dick Merrill looked and acted like a north woods guide was supposed to look and act.. Kinda like John Wayne looked like a cowboy is supposed to look.

Last but not least was Bud Seeley. Bud was just getting into the guiding game, but did what was expected of him and asked a lot of good questions. He'd do just fine.

And then, there was Dad and me. As for me, I was just about as important as the fig leaf in the story of Adam and Eve.

Mr. Duetch had an on going custom when ever he brought up a group of anglers on a fishing trip. First, he'd have the guys pair up. This was done by drawing numbers out of a hat or cards from a deck. If there was an odd number of persons, such as this trip, one member of the group would end up without a companion. Next, Mr. Duetch would put the names of all the guides in a hat and each team of fishermen would draw a name to see who there guide would be. Well, the plan didn't quite work that way on my first official day of guiding.

Mom and I were in the kitchen preparing breakfast for the Duetch Gang well before they began filing into our dining room. Dad remained in the dining area to greet and seat our clients. Once settled into their chairs, Mr. Duetch proceeded with his program. After all the drawings had been completed I heard one of the members issue a complaint. Loud and clear.

"I ain't gonna come up north and spend all my money on a fishing trip and then get stuck with some sixteen year old rookie guide!" My elated exuberance took a rapid nosedive!

An awkward silence followed. Then one of Mr. Duetch's long time followers spoke up. Equally loud and clear.

"I'll fish with Buckshot. I'll take the kid. I'll fish alone with him. He'll do just fine. I DON'T have a problemwith him." My yet to be established reputation was saved, at least for the moment.

When the week end was over, and all the fish were counted, my boat came in second! You can probably guess who came in first. Yep, Dad!

After our week end guests had left, Dad told me Mr. Duetch had taken the disgruntled complainer aside and given him a tongue lashing that nearly drew blood. And that fisherman was never again invited to be a member of "Duetch's Gang". I often wondered if he had learned his lesson on the subject of complaining about the merchandise before it was tested.

Well, anyway, my guiding career had been successfully launched. I was only able to guide four days in May of '53. With high school still in session and me playing second base for the Eagle River High School baseball team, I had to put any serious attempts to do more guiding on the back burner until school let out. That blessed even took place on May 29th.

By the time June 27th rolled around, I had chalked up fourteen more guiding dates. Not too shabby for a rookie. And then my two good buddies from Chicago, Johnny and Eddie, arrived. (See; "EVERY LAKE NEEDS SOME CLAMS")

Johnny and Eddie arrived with their dad and uncle to spend nine days fishing in the fabled north woods. Dad had guided Mr. Petras many times since their first meeting in 1945. Also, Johnny, Eddie and I had spent many hours together fishing for whatever might happen to attack our hooks. But now, I was going to be "their guide" for nine days in a row! I would actually be getting $7.50 a day for havin' fun and helping them catch some fish! I was in hog heaven! This guidin' was O.K.!

From June 27th through June 29th we fished Lake Laura and Plum Crick. In those three days my clients and I landed twenty one nice sized bass, two walleyes and thirty three brook trout. Not bad for a boat load of teenagers! During those same three days Dad and his clients, Johnny and Eddie's dad and uncle, landed sixteen bass and three walleyes. The kids had out fished the "pros". Thus proving that miracles do happen occasionally.

And then it was June 30, 1953.

The senior guide decided the six of us would have another go at those wonderful deep water bass and walleyes that inhabited the pristine waters of Lake Laura. No one objected. After one of Mom's gut filling breakfasts we stopped in Sayner to buy some minnows from Joe Froelich, who specialized in having the freshest, choicest, black chubs in captivity. It was here we learned the weather forecasters were warning of possible severe weather for our area later in the day. I didn't pay much attention to the warning.

Dad launched his boat at what was known as the "east landing", which was close to the "hot weed bed" where our clients had been catching most of those nice sized bass and walleye. As for me, I had not yet saved enough money to buy a boat and motor, so I was forced to rent a boat from Lawrence Ellerman. Mr. Ellerman had several nice rowing boats for rent, which were moored at what was called the "west landing" on Lake Laura. So I had to spend one dollar of the seven fifty I was earning each day for a boat to fish from. But I didn't care. After all fishin' and guidin' was more fun than makin' money anyway. (And you know what? Over fifty years later I still feel the same way!)

By the time we unloaded the car, stashed all our gear in the boat, and attached the outboard motor Mr. Petras has loaned us, it was nearing 8:30 a.m. Arriving at the "hot weed bed" a few minutes later we noted that Dad and his clients were well on the way to securing a nice stringer of bass and walleye. I guess they had decided it was time to get serious, as the kids were getting big heads.

For me, having an outboard motor was quite a luxury. Generally I had to row from spot to spot, or if I was on the same lake as Dad, sometimes he'd tow me with his 1.8 horse power ancient Johnson Sea Horse. But today my boat contained a 7.5 h.p. Mercury, which was nearly new. And boy oh boy did that big motor make our boat fly. In fact, having that big motor was one of the reasons we weren't doing so good in the fish catching department. We were too busy roaring from one "hot spot" to another.

Dad had done a great job trying to teach me as much as he could about guiding. My instruction had included a chapter concerning dangerous weather situations. I had been warned repeatedly about two particularly warnings that Mother Nature usually gave prior to nasty or severe weather. And both of these warnings meant "GET OFF THE LAKE, NOW!"

Warning number one would be thunder and/or lightning. Warning number two would be dark or discolored clouds that moved AGAINST the direction of the surface wind. June 30, 1953 would produce both "one" and "two" category warnings!

It was about ten o'clock when the western sky began to signal the first warning of an impending disaster. Thick, black clouds began to gather and slowly moved in our direction. AGAINST a gentle east wind. But those clouds were a long way off and we were catching a few nice sized bass. And those bass were striking our bait with a vengeance! Knowing that fish generally feed ferociously preceding a storm or cold front, we began fishing more intently.

A half hour passed. Looking at the gathering storm clouds I noted they had changed colors. The dark, black clouds now contained streaks of yellow, purple and a sickly looking shade of green. I had never seen such weird clouds! And those clouds were still moving slowly eastward. The fish began to bite even better!

A few minutes after eleven o'clock a distant rumble of thunder brought our eyes back to those clouds. They were swirling now, and seemed to have moved a great deal closer to us in a short period of time. And then the easterly wind died as though it had been shut off with a switch. An eerie silence descended over Lake Laura. Now the entire western sky was colored a dirty, jaundiced yellow. From the western end of the lake a new sound reached our ears. Wind! Strong wind!

Even from a distance of nearly a mile, we could see the surface of the lake begin to ripple. The ripples soon increased to a field of white tipped waves. I knew I had waited too long. I should have been on the shore by now, or at least heading in that direction. I looked all around for Dad's boat, but could not locate it. Several other boat loads of anglers were still fishing the weed bed, but Dad was nowhere to be seen. I guessed that he was already at the east landing, safe and sound. I gave the order to get off the water!

By the time I had pulled our minnow bucket and stringer of fish into the boat, Johnny had his dad's Mercury going full speed toward the west landing. The wind met us before we had motored a hundred yards! And it was blowing with great force. Foam crested white caps crashed over the bow of our boat as we sliced through the rapidly growing waves. The cool spray actually felt good on our faces and arms as the distance between our boat and the landing narrowed.

By the time we reached the dock it had begun pouring rain, and thundering like the Battle of the Bulge. It appeared we were experiencing "The Mother of all Storms". Little did we know it was about to get much worse!

It took but a few minutes for the three of us to move our equipment from the boat to the trunk of our car. But before departing for home I needed to fill our minnow bucket with fresh water. Good chubs cost money and we'd need them later in the day when the storm blew over and we once again could return to our fishing.

I hurried to the dock and filled our minnow bucket with fresh water. I was about to return to the dry interior of our car when a sudden violent gust of wind nearly blew me into Lake Laura. Gusts of winds were causing sheets of rain to fall more horizontally than vertical. Raindrops were pelting me so hard it felt like I was being bombarded with hail stones. By the time I regained the safety of our car the wind was shrieking worse than a soprano in an Italian opera, And now the rain was falling so heavily we were unable to see the opposite shore of the lake. But something else we couldn't see was a whirling funnel of death, churning eastward less than a hundred yards from shore!

Johnny was behind the wheel as we slowly began to inch ourselves along the narrow dirt road that would lead us to County Highway K, which was a little over a mile distance. The rain was pounding earthward so violently our windshield wipers could not keep the windshield clear. We had driven but several hundred feet when a gigantic sugar maple crashed to the ground, just missing the front of our vehicle! We had no choice but to stay were we were until the storm passed. At the time we had no idea our car would be staying where it was for over three hours.

Above the whine and roar of the storm we could hear the cracking and crashing of trees being uprooted or snapped off like match sticks. But from the inside of the fogged up interior of our car we could see nothing but raindrops and leaves bouncing off our windows and windshield. Several times our car shuddered, as though it might become airborne. Never had any of us experienced such violence in a storm. And then,...suddenly it was over.

Slowly we eased ourselves out of the stuffy interior of the car and looked around. The sight that greeted our eyes was beyond belief! The west landing, and the forest around it as far as we could see, looked as though a squadron of B-29's had bombed the area. Downed trees and twisted limbs were strewn in every direction. Millions of wet, green leaves littered the forest floor. From the trees that had survived the onslaught, water dripped like a thousand leaking faucets. We stood in mute silence with our mouths hanging open in disbelief. And then we noticed we were not alone.

The half dozen or so other vehicles that occupied the cramped parking area next to the landing also contained survivors. Most were out of town tourists. Some had small children with them. Some were nearly hysterical. But no one was injured. Or worse! It was time to do something positive about our situation.

Moving the giant old maple was out of the question. It was over two feet in diameter. It weighed tons. And not one vehicle hand any tools that could have helped move the tree or cut it up in manageable pieces. There was but one course of action. Someone would have to walk the mile and a quarter to Highway K and get help. "Someone" was Johnny, Eddie and I.

There were over thirty trees of various sizes blocking the road between the west landing on Lake Laura and Highway K. But they were but a minor fraction of the tens of thousands that were downed in Vilas County that fateful day of destruction. It took less than a half hour for the three of us to reach the highway.

Located at the junction of the dirt road that led us from the landing to Highway K, is a tavern and cafe. At the time it was owned by a couple who were good friends of Dad and Mom. Their names were Mr. & Mrs. Stazik. I explained the situation that existed at Lake Laura and asked if they could phone for help. Their phone was dead. Also, they were without electricity.

Later, we discovered that hundreds of other households also were without those services. So, we borrowed an ax and a cross cut saw and began the monumental task of clearing the road. Help arrived a half hour later.

We were bulling our way through tree number five, huffing and puffing, pulling on that old dull cross cut saw, when an orange truck pulled in behind us. It was the work crew from the Township of Plum Lake who had been clearing downed trees off Highway K. The crew had stopped at Stazik's Tavern and were informed about all the people who were stranded at the west landing on Lake Laura.

With five of us now clearing the downed trees, the task became much easier. The town crew didn't need to huff and puff pulling a dull cross cut saw. They had one of those new fangled machines called a "chain saw". And boy could that thing saw! In less than two hours the road was re-opened and the stranded vacationers were freed from their temporary prison.

Once again homeward bound, Johnny, Eddie and I began to realize the enormous amount of damage the storm had inflicted on central and south Vilas County. The trip from Lake Laura to Kasomo Lodge usually took about fifteen minutes. On June 30, 1953 it took over a half hour. All along our route on Highways K, N, 155, and C, were hundreds of downed trees, plus numerous telephone and electric poles. Town and County work crews, plus many citizens and vacationers, were in the process of helping to open the roads to traffic. In several places we had to drive around fallen trees to reach our destination. It was nearing 3:30 p.m. before we achieved our goal. Mom had some questions to ask.

"Where did you and your father fish today?"

"We were on Lake Laura. And boy oh boy, did we ever have a storm!"

"Where is your father now?"

"Back on Lake Laura, I guess. He used the east landing and we used the west landing. The last time I saw him was just before the storm hit."

"OH MY GOD! You better go back and look for him. I've been listening to our battery powered radio and the newscaster said a tornado hit Lake Laura,... and,... four persons are missing! Go find your father!"

Caution was thrown to the wind as we raced back towards Lake Laura as quickly as possible. There was a lump in my throat the size of a watermelon. None of us said much, but each of us knew what the others were thinking. Our dads and Johnny and Eddie's uncle were out there somewhere, and the news Mom had related to us caused a deep feeling of foreboding. Our journey back to Lake Laura seemed to last an eternity and our minds were filled with fear.

The parking area at the east landing was filled with official and emergency vehicles of all types. Squad cars from the Vilas County Sheriff's Department. An ambulance. The coroner. Two Department of Natural

Resources trucks. Plus numerous curious onlookers. It was difficult to locate a place to park.

On the beach lay two bodies, covered with wool blankets. Further out on the lake two DNR boats were slowly combing the lake bottom with grappling hooks, trying to locate the two remaining bodies of the four victims that had perished in the tornado. But who were they?

"PLEASE", I silently prayed, "not my Dad! Please God, not my Dad!" Our worst fears were magnified by the sight before us. But then I looked further out on the now peaceful surface of Lake Laura. I saw something that made my heart leap!

About a half mile away I sighted a familiar green Thompson Guide Boat, slowly rising and falling in the gentle waves. And there were three adult men fishing as if nothing out of the ordinary had taken place. Yep, that was my Dad's style alright. Just keep doin' your job till it done.

Johnny, Eddie and I slapped each other on the back, raced for our car and headed home. The return trip to Kasomo Lodge was a lot brighter, and the trip seemed a lot shorter.

By evening the full extent of the disaster began to become known. Dad, plus Johnny and Eddie's dad and uncle, were able to relate a blow by blow account of what happened when the killer tornado touched down on Lake Laura.

There was a good reason why I hadn't seen Dad's boat when I foolishly headed west, into the teeth of the oncoming storm. He had left the weed bed we had been fishing and rowed a considerable distance to the north shore to fish on a rock bar that was located there. I just hadn't looked in the right place. Dad had watched us depart but was unable to warn us of my stupid decision.

Then he too had started motoring towards the east landing, as he knew full well a major storm was getting close. He and his clients had not motored far when Dad saw the tornado touch down on the west end of the lake. Knowing full well his little 1.8 h.p. outboard would never beat the storm, he switched to Plan B.

By now, the whirling mass of wind and water was bearing down on the east end of the lake. Directing his boat to the nearest shore, Dad stopped his boat in water that was armpit deep and ordered his two companions to jump into the lake. The three of them clung to the boat as the tornado sped closer and closer. It was then they saw two other boats, filled with vacationers,... heading east.

There were nine people and a dog jammed into two small, flat bottomed boats. The lead boat was powered by a small outboard motor with four persons aboard. It was towing a second boat, overloaded with five persons and a dog. The occupants seemed unaware of the snarling twister bearing down on them. The two boats passed within a few hundred feet of Dad and his clients, who were hunkered down in the water, waiting for the onslaught. Dad yelled and waved his old felt hat at the innocent by-passers, trying to get their attention to warn them of the impending danger. The diver of the outboard waved back and continued eastward. Four of the nine people had only minutes to live!

The conclusion of the story is tragic. The two boats somehow became separated in the raging cyclone. To this day the truth of how that separation occurred is not known. At least it is not known to the general public. Two versions of what happened surfaced. Perhaps neither is true.

One version states that the second boat capsized, and the rope which was being used to tow it broke. The storm was so violent that the motor driven boat was unable to turn back and attempt a rescue.

The second version rumored that the driver of the motor driven boat cut the tow rope in order to save himself and the three others with him.

But whatever happened, four persons were dead. The victims included a mother, her infant child, and the child's grandmother and grandfather. A young boy was somehow able to cling to the overturned boat until he was rescued after the twister left the lake. The dog swam to shore.

The following day we learned that the killer storms had claimed a fifth victim. A young boy, staying at a boys camp on Plum Lake was killed when a large tree fell on the tent in which he was staying. He was impaled by one of the tree's branches.

It was determined that at least three different twisters struck Vilas County between eleven a.m. and one p.m. Possibly more. There certainly was one that churned its way across Lake Laura. A second twister struck Razorback and Plum Lakes. A third tornado was sighted dancing across Lost Lake. And stranger still, every tree on a small island on Frank Lake was flattened, while not another single tree or shrub was damaged anywhere else on the entire lake! Strange are the feats of Mother Nature.

The damage was estimated to be in the millions of dollars. Resorts on Plum Lake and Razorback Lake were severely damaged. Trees fell and crushed automobiles, cottages and homes. Boats, boat houses, and personal property of all types were wrecked or simply missing. Hundreds of telephone and power lines were down. Much of the county was without these services. Acres and acres of beautiful forest land had been flattened. But worst of all were the deaths of five innocent persons. It was indeed fortunate that there hadn't been more deaths.

Electricity and phone service would not be functioning again for hundreds of homes and businesses for from three to five days. Kasomo Lodge suffered for four days. Much of the food in our freezer had to be discarded, as we couldn't eat it as fast as it thawed out and spoiled.

However, Johnny, Eddie and I, through a valiant effort which required much suffering on our part, disposed of four gallons of ice cream before it turned to mush.

Dad and his clients returned to the waters of Lake Laura the day following the disaster and added seven bass and three walleyes to the thirteen fish they had boated during "The Day of the Twister". As for Johnny, Eddie and I, we spent the next two days driving around the county viewing all the damage. And feeling very lucky we weren't part of the final grim statistics. By July 3rd we were once again catching fish.

We were lucky to have survived, considering we were not mature enough to realize it is not wise to try to beat a storm by heading INTO it. A nearly fatal mistake that I have never made again. Nor do I ever plan on trying it again! I have often felt it may have been Mr. Petras' 7.5 h.p. Mercury motor that saved our lives that terrible day on Lake Laura!

So,...all things considered, I chalked June 30, 1953 up as another of life's learning experiences. I realized all too well, "Don't mess with Mother Nature. She's much tougher that you are!"

# "Charlie" The (almost) Guide

Dad Anderson undertook many highly difficult jobs in his lifetime. When Dad tackled a job, he put all his heart and soul into getting that job done, and done well! Most of his finished products were highly satisfactory. But there was one project Dad attempted, which dragged out over a period of several years,...but never reached completion. In fact, the project ended up in utter failure. However, during the course of this ill fated attempt, the project supplied the Anderson Family, as well as dozens of other individuals, a lifetime of memories. And quite a few laughs. A half century later I still have to chuckle at the memories!

Charlie, Charlie, Charlie! God Rest Your Soul! Charlie passed away a few years ago at the ripe old age of ninety three. Yes sir, he was a tough old bird. He was also a super human being, possessing a kind and gentle spirit, (unless you damaged his car) and was counted among my dearest of friends. But like all human beings,...he did have a few shortcomings!

In several of my earlier attempts at literature, you have already been introduced to *"Charlie"*. You suffered with him during his introduction to fishing for trout and camping in an earlier tale, "Once Upon The Pine". Charlie also played a bit part in my ramblings entitled "For Ducks, It Was Devine", and "Brule Barrens Sharptails, and More". But to have known Charlie was to love the man. Even in times of failure. Especially if the act of failing offered a laugh or two.

As I indicated earlier, in "Once Upon The Pine", Dad and Charlie became best of friends shortly after World War II ended when Charlie and his wife, Rosemary, moved to the north woods from Chicago. The north woods of the '40's and '50's was a much different place than it is today. (And of course, I can't think of many places that wouldn't fit that same description.) So, having said that, to completely understand what I am going to tell you in the following two paragraphs, the reader must understand a tad of north woods history. I will be brief.

The north woods of Wisconsin was opened to substantial settlement by non-Native Americans with the beginning of vast logging operations, which began in earnest during the late 1860's and early 1870's. The "Great Chicago Fire" provided the catalyst which fueled the raping of the north's virgin pine timber. One historian declared, "Chicago was rebuilt after the fire of 1871 with the sweat and blood of the north woods lumberjacks." I have no doubt that he was correct. The "hay day" of the logging industry lasted but a scant half century. By the time the mid 1920's rolled around, ninety nine per-cent of all the virgin pine was gone. Forever!

Some former loggers tried their hand at farming the ravaged land, but the g rowing season was too short and the soil was too poor to support much agriculture. Some kept the wolf away from their door by trapping. Some had the foresight to attempt to promote tourism. Most moved away. Slowly, but steadily, the tourism industry gained momentum. And by the late 1950's tourism was the life blood of the north woods. So it continues to this day. But the important fact the reader must know and understand is this. From the end of the logging era through the late 1950's, the north woods was in a deep, perpetual, economic depression!

For any "newcomers". who immigrated to the peace and beauty of the north woods, most discovered they had jumped into something that was much different from what they had envisioned! Life was good, but it was also tough. Very tough! And sometime brutal. To survive, one needed to adapt to this land, with it's often hostile environment and limited economic opportunities! Newcomers, as well as the "natives" had to be made of strong will and strong back. Usually, the only person one could rely on to solve their many problems were themselves. Failure to become a "jack of all trades" usually resulted in an inability to survive economically. Those "newcomers" who were befriended by an established "local", and had the insight to take the advise offered by that new friend, had the best chance to survive.

Shortly after World War II. Charlie and Rose bought a resort on Big St. Germain Lake. Both were very hard workers and were fortunate to have a respectable reserve of financial support in the bank prior to moving north.

With the war years behind us, the tourist industry in the north woods exploded like fall mushrooms after a warm rain. The roads and highways leading north were chocked with "down staters" and "out of staters" from Memorial Day through Labor Day. It was a short tourist season, so it was necessary to "make hay while the sun shined". The tourists had the hay and the folks living in the north wood had better have a sharp sickle. North woods residents needed to harvest fast,...and often! As Dad Anderson aptly stated, "Winter up here lasts nine months."

Most resort were able to keep their cottages booked fairly solid through July and August. June was "iffy", due to it's uncertain mood swings. One year June could be beautiful, the next season could be cold and rainy. Plus many of the city schools didn't shut down until mid June. May and September offered a dribble of money, but once the schools opened for business around Labor Day, most resort owners boarded up the windows and began to get ready for those nine months of winter.

The most enterprising local bumpkins, besides renting cabins to the tourists, tried to devise additional ploys to help lighten the tourist's wallets. However, that was a tough assignment. During the infancy of tourism in the north woods, there was but mainly two things to do while on vacation. Relax and fish. And generally the two went hand in hand. Unlike today's visitors, who have a multitude of varied activities to keep them busy, vacationing in the north woods was mostly peace and quiet. Walks in the woods on well marked, well maintained hiking trails. A canoe ride on a pristine lake at sunset. Reading a book in a giant hammock stretched between two bushy shade trees. A cooling dip in a gin clear lake, then warming up by snuggling into warm beach sand. Bonding with friends and family around an evening campfire. And fishing. That was the usual agenda.

Bringing your own boat north for vacationing purposes was unheard of. Most people didn't own a boat. Each resort provided a boat with each cottage. Usually no motor, but outboards were cantankerous, noisy smoke belching monsters anyway. Rowing was good exercise. For the anglers of the period, there were no lake maps to pin point the "hot spots". The depth finder/fish locator had not as yet been invented. And even though the lakes teemed with fish, the average tourist didn't have the faintest idea of how to successfully fill his stringer with a limit of walleye, bass, northern, or even panfish.

Enter the "Northwood's Fishing Guide"

There had been a smattering of tourism in the north woods dating back to the early 1880's. The birth of the "Northwood's Fishing Guide" was a natural evolution, coinciding with the birth of the tourist industry. But there were never enough tourists to keep many guides working steady all summer,...until the end of World War II. Then it didn't take long for the demand to outstrip the supply.

With the end of the war, trains and autos brought hoards of vacationing fishermen from cities like Chicago, Milwaukee, Minneapolis, St. Louis, and a host of other urban area, some as far away as New York and California! These eager anglers gathered in various resorts and "fishing camps" scattered throughout the north woods. And for thousands of these nimrods, the north woods became the destination for their "Annual Fishing Trip". Some groups and individuals scheduled multiple fishing trips throughout the tourist season. It was these large groups of men, usually well to do executives from prestigious corporations and businesses, that required more and more guides to fill their needs. So it became the obligation of the "veteran" guides to secure and train new ones. Enter "Charlie", stage center!

Dad Anderson had already begun the task of trying to train Charlie so he might more thoroughly enjoy his new found environment. And also add to his ability of surviving in the north wood's harsh economic climate. Dad took Charlie fishing, hunting, and camping. He showed Charlie how to cut wood, fix leaky toilets, repair leaky boats, locate and fix leaks in cabin roofs and patch leady waders. There was lots of stuff that leaked in those days.

And even though Charlie didn't catch on right away to everything Dad tried to teach him, Charlie was a good student and tried real hard to master those necessary skills.

So it was that Dad decided to take Charlie under his wing and try to teach him the basics of the guiding profession. On the surface, Charlie looked like a natural. He was intelligent. He had an outgoing, friendly, personality. He was a hard worker. He liked to fish. And,...he really liked making money! But,...he was a bit shy about spending much. The lessons began.

Lesson One: "Obtaining a License to Guide"

Call the DNR Office in Madison for an application. Fill in your age, weight, height, hair color and address. Are you a citizen of Wisconsin? "Yes" Have you been convicted of any fish or game violations in the last three years? "No" Sign here and enclose one dollar. Easy assignment!

Lesson Two: "Obtaining a Good, Dependable Outboard Motor"

It was at this early stage of Charlie's schooling that Charlie's conservative nature, (ie, spending money) cropped up. As Charlie and Dad viewed a selection of outboard motors at "Froelich's Hardware Store" in Sayner, WI., the dialog between teacher and student went something like this.

"Well Charlie, here's the kind of outboard motor you should buy. This is a brand new, sweet little three horse power Johnson Sea Horse."

Charlie looked at the price tag. $89.50. Charlie's brow furrowed. "How come a Johnson costs so much?"

"Well, they're the best motor money can buy. They're dependable, they start easily and require very little maintenance. Just think of the one on my boat. It's a 1928 model that I paid twenty five bucks for ten years ago, and I ain't had one lick of trouble with it. A guide needs a dependable motor. One that will take a lickin' and keep on tickin. Har de har har!"

Charlie looked skeptical. "Well,...I don't know Andy. Eighty nine fifty is a lot of green. Maybe I'll look around at some other brands and make some comparisons."

One of Charlie's shortcomings had reared its ugly head!

So, Charlie shopped around and bought a seven and a half house power outboard from one of the popular mail order catalogs. It was on sale for $65.00, plus shipping. Charlie was pretty happy about his purchase. He had the biggest motor of any guide within a hundred mile radius, and he had saved about fifteen bucks. Also, Charlie's new motor was one of those long shaft models. The longer shaft would put the propeller about a foot deeper into the water than those little 3 h.p. Johnson motors.

Lesson Three: "Obtaining the PROPER and Necessary Equipment"

A couple of weeks prior to the opening of fishing season, Dad took Charlie to "Spiess' Sporting Goods Store" in downtown Eagle River, WI. The conversation went something like this.

"Well Charlie, here's the rack of rods. I'd recommend this Heddon Pal Musky Special. It's just like the one I've been using for years and years. They're the top of the line!"

Charlie looked at the price tag. $16.95. "Wow! Sixteen ninety five is a lot of green. What about this one over here? It looks almost like the Heddon Pal and it's only $3.98!"

"Naw, don't buy that piece of junk. That's a Wondo-Semi-Flex and it won't last the summer. Hook one good musky or get snagged on a log and it'll bust."

"Ya, but I'll be saving $12.97!"

Charlie bought the Wondo-Semi-Flex. Next item.

"O.K. Charlie, here's the display case full of reels. I'd get the Pflueger Supreme. It's just like the ones all the guides use. They hardly ever wear out and if they do give you a problem, just send her back to the company and they'll fix her up for free!" Dad was trying hard to play on Charlie's conservative nature.

Charlie looked at the price tag. $24.95. "Holdy smokes! The reel cost more than the rods! Twenty four ninety five is a lot of green! What about these cheaper models?"

"Now listen Charlie. This is importat. If there's one piece of equipment you don't want to chinch on, it's a reel. They take a real beating! Har de har har! Pardon the pun. Take it from me, if you buy anything else but a Pflueger, you're asking for trouble."

Charlie purchased a "Wondo-Knuckle-Buster" for $6,75.

"Andy, this one looks real good. And I saved $18.20.!"

The trend continued through the remaining purchases. Fishing line. Buy some new braded nylon for $1.98? Nope. The old silk line only costs 59 cents. Buy the canvas covered boat cushions for $3.79? Nope. Spend $1.89 for the plastic covered ones. By Eagle Claw or Webber hooks? Nope. The cheaper mustads will do the job. And on and on it went. The final item that needed to be purchased was a minnow bucket.

"O.K. Charlie, here's the minnow buckets stacked on that top shelf over there. Buy one of those on the left. It's a good galvanized one that floats."

Charlie looked at the price tag. $2.95. "Hummmmm, why is the one on the left two ninety five and the one on the right looks identical for only one ninety five?"

"The one on the right doesn't float."

"Why do you need one that floats?"

"Because if it comes untied from your boat, it will sink. You'll not only loose the inside part of the bucket, but you'll also loose all your expensive minnows."

"Well, I was in the Boy Scouts and I know how to tie a good knot."

Charlie bought the sinker. And he saved another dollar!

On the ride back to St. Germain, Dad was rather quiet. I could see the wheels turning in his head. I had also detected the first glimmer of doubt in his eyes. Doubt that his new project, which was trying to mold Charlie into a good guide, was going to be successful. Dad always had a keen ability to foresee the outcome of most events during the early stages of development,...or in this case, lack of development.

Charlie, on the other hand, was bubbling over with happiness. "Wow, Andy! It sure was nice of you to help me pick out all that stuff I'll need to started guiding. Even though I didn't buy any of the equipment you suggested,... well, I probably won't be guiding as much as you do,...so I probably really don't need equipment as expensive as yours. And you know what? I saved $63.76 by not buying the brands you suggested." Charlie was awful good in math.

Dad grinned, but it wasn't one of his genuine grins!

Charlie's first major problem with his bargain equipment occurred one beautiful June morning on Allequash Lake. A half dozen guides, with their clients on board, were strung out in the channel between lower and upper Allequash, heading for the lush weeds beds of the upper lake. Charlie, being the "rookie" guide was last in line. The channel in question is about three hundred yards in length, averaging about a foot and a half deep, the bottom being comprised mostly of muck. Except for three shallow veins of gravel and rock near the entrance to the upper lake. By running an outboard slowly, like the small Johnson or Evinrude models, there is no chance of striking bottom with the propeller. That is because the Johnson and Evinrude motors have SHORT shafts.

Closely watching the line of boats ahead of him, Charlie saw the guides increase their speed as they neared the channel's opening into upper Allequash. Charlie opened the throttle of his high powered seven and a half horse, LONG SHAFT, "catalog special". Disaster was only seconds away!

Unknown to Charlie, the third vein of gravel and large boulders was still slightly ahead of his boat. The propeller of his long shaft outboard discovered several of the boulders, which were just slightly smaller than Mount Everest.

BANG! CRUNCH! GRIND! POW! WHAM! SMASH! And finally, POP! The "POP" was the lower unit of Charlie's outboard tearing loose from the shaft. Now he had a short shaft motor,...minus the propeller. He sure looked silly, sitting with his hand on the throttle, the engine roaring at full speed, but this boat wasn't moving. Charlie got to do a lot of rowing that day.

As the summer wore on Charlie's list of disasters grew longer. Also, his "savings" of $63.76 evaporated and actually landed on the minus side after he paid the bill to have his lower unit replaced.

The 59 cent silk line was the major contributor to Disaster Number Two. The events leading up to his line's final gasp resulted in one of the funniest fishing stories ever recorded from the lake of the fabled north woods. The "Three Stooges" would have been impressed. The comedy of errors unfolded thusly.

Several boats, loaded with clients and their guides, were combing a large weed bed on Big St. Germain Lake. Charlie's client did not have a rod and reel, so Charlie loaned him his "Wondo-Semi-Flex" rod and "Wondo-Knuckle-Buster" reel. The reel contained what remained of the spool of 59 cent silk line. Charlie's client hooked into a northern pike of trophy size. The hook was set and the battle commenced.

The client would gain some line, then give some back, to let the monster run and tire himself. Back and forth the battle raged. The occupants of the neighboring boats put down their rods to watch the epic contest. Words of advise and encouragement echoed across the water. Charlie, with a William Penn nickel cigar clenched in his teeth, readied the net. Slowly the finny gladiator weakened. Inch by begrudging inch the toothy denizen of the deep began to surrender. Charlie leaned out over the edge of the boat to get in position for the final coup de grace. Victory was in sight!

The nearly spent northern was now slowly swimming parallel to the boat. Suddenly, the gallant fish sensed danger! Gathering it's last ounce of strength, the fearful monster put the peddle to the metal. Charlie, surprised by the fish's sudden burst of speed, leaned further over the rail of his boat and made a quick lunge at the fish with the net.

Only the fishermen in the boat closest to Charlie's boat actually saw what happened next. A small puff of cigar ash exploded in Charlie's face. The "Wondo-Semi-Flex" rod, which had been bent nearly double during the conflict, snapped upward. The burned end of what was left of Charlie's 59 cent silk line fluttered in the soft breeze. The client, now holding a fishless rod, yelled, "What the hell happened?"

Charlie, sputtering and wiping cigar ashes out of his eyes, attempted to bamboozle the city slicker. "It busted the line. You were putting too much pressure on him!"

But from the onlookers in the next boat, who were roaring with laugher, came the correct explanation. "Hey Charlie, the line touched the end of your cigar and burned it in two. Too bad, but silk does that. You should have been using nylon line. Nylon would have held." And at days end,...there was no tip for Charlie.

By season's end, Charlie's "Wondo-Knuckle-Buster" reel sounded like a coffee grinder full of small stones.

The "Wondo-Semi-Flex" rod was somehow still in one piece, but the cork covering the handle had be re-glued to the rod several times. All three plastic covered boat cushions were torn and leaking kapok, which is the flotation material. And his outboard motor was smoking so heavily it actually would rid the area around a lake of mosquitoes! Well, not quite that bad. But Charlie was undaunted by his equipment's failure, and looked forward to the coming summer and his second season of guiding.

Things got off to a rough start for Charlie the following spring. Upon removing his rod and reel from the closet where he had stored them during the winter, Charlie discovered more trouble. The gears in his reel had rusted so badly the reel handle wouldn't budge. His fishing pole had acquired a permanent warp, making it look more like a bow for shooting arrows than a fishing rod. Funerals were held. Charlie purchased a Heddon Pal Musky Special and a Pflueger Supreme reel. And nylon line.

The demise of Charlie's final piece of original equipment took place one lovely June morning on Lake Laura. Dad, Charlie and myself were guiding a group of anglers from Cincinnati, Ohio. Dad had guided for this group many times, I a few times, and this was Charlie's first.

We located large numbers of bass and walleye in a deep weed bed several hundred yards off the southwest shore. Our stringers were rapidly being filled with nice sized fish, as our clients "ho, hoed" and "hee hawed", having the time of their lives. But then Dad and I noticed an eerie silence hanging over Charlie's boat. And Charlie was slowly rowing in our direction. As he pulled up besides Dad's boat, his face containing a serious look. Charlie took the nickel William Penn out of his mouth and spoke.

"Say Andy, could I borrow a couple dozen minnows?"

"What? Have you used up all five dozen already? We've only been fishing for an hour!"

"Well,...ah,...ahem," Charlie stammered, "I lost my minnow bucket."

"What do you mean, lost your minnow bucket?"

"Well,...ah,...ahem,...My knot came untied and it sunk."

"HO, HO, HO, HAW, HAW, HAW, HEE, HEE, HEE," roared Dad, tears streaming down his ruddy red face. "I figured that'd happen sooner or later! HAR, HAR, DE, HAR, HAR HAR!"

Well, Dad and I each gave Charlie a few minnows, which he was forced to store in a coffee can that was usually used as his boat's emergency rest room. That brought out a few more HAR, DE, HAR, HARS from everyone in all three boats,...except Charlie. He was re-lighting his William Penn.

Of course, all the gentlemen in the fishing party wanted to know what was so outrageously funny about loosing a minnow bucket and four dollars worth of choice chubs. So Dad told them about Charlie opting to save a buck by not buying a minnow bucket that would float. Charlie's face looked red.

Summer flitted by, as summers have the habit of doing, and Charlie seemed to be catchin' on to learning how to guide,... little by little. But Dad said he didn't think Charlie was really havin' fun when he did it. Guidin' I mean.

Labor Day arrived, and as usual most all the tourists vacated the north woods. Dad and I put our boats and all our guidin' equipment in storage. And I started my senior year of high school.

It was Christmas when the final chapter was written concerning Charlie's sunken minnow bucket. Charlie received a large, heavy package which had been sent from an address in Cincinnati, Ohio. Wondering what the box contained, and who had sent it, Charlie wasted no time in tearing it open.

Inside the box was twenty five feet of fairly heavy chain, with snaps on both ends. There was also a note.

> Dear Charlie,
>
> Recently I was telling some friends about our day
> of fishing on Lake Laura last June, and I got a wonderful
> idea for a gift, which is enclosed. Attach one end of this
> chain to your boat, and the other end to your minnow
> bucket.
> Then, when your Boy Scout knot comes untied, just pull on
> the chain and retrieve your bucket full of minnows.
>
> > With kindest regards,
> > Joe Hales

POSTSCRIPT: Charlie did a little more guiding over the next two summers, but then retired from the profession. Dad told Charlie why he never made it as a guide.

"Charlie, I think because you are left handed and were born and raised in Chicago is why you weren't able to master the skills necessary to become a guide. HAR, DE, HAR, HAR HAR!"

Quite often I was amazed Charlie and Dad remained such good friends.

# Of Men, Ducks, and a Double Barreled Shotgun

It was late September and Uncle Bud was in a rip roaring foul mood. And all because there was a lack of fowl. Ruffed grouse, partridge, woods chicken, or whatever you know them by were in the lowest ebb of their population cycle. Uncle Bud knew it too, but he was still in a foul mood about the situation. His grumbling was relentless!

"Ain't seen a feather in the last week. Hunted most of the good cover all the way to Escanaba Lake and back and never saw a bird. Even took Old Pat with me and plowed through the alders along Plum Crick. Nothin' there either. A guy waits all year for partridge season, and then there ain't none to shoot at.

Dad, Mom and me were gettin' pretty tired of listenin' to Uncle Bud's ranting and ravin' every night at the dinner table. The lack of grouse seemed to be the only thing on his mind. Dad tried to change the subject.

"Well, you know good and well that partridge populations go in cycles. They go from high to low about every seven years. And this is the low end of the cycle. Nothin' we can do about it. But look at the bright side. The mallards and black ducks had three broods this summer and the country is chin deep with ducks. The season opens Saturday after next. Buckshot, Charlie and me were over to Devine yesterday fixin' up our blinds and we saw hundreds of ducks. Why don't you come along with us and hunt ducks. You used to hunt with us once in awhile. We always have a good time. What'd ya say?"

"Don't care much for duck. Don't like dark meat. Don't like sleepin' in that stinkin' canvas tent. Don't like gettin' up at four a.m. Don't like ridin' in Charlie's canoe. It's too tippy. Besides, I don't have a 12 gauge shotgun for duck huntin' anymore. You know I traded her off for that little 20 gauge pump, which is better for huntin' partridge." As I said, Uncle Bud was in a foul mood!

Uncle Bud and me got along real good. Next to Mom and Dad, Uncle Bud was my favorite person in the whole world. Being a bachelor, he had lived with us most of my short life. He was an ace carpenter, and had been a great asset helping Dad and Mom build our resort and fix stuff that got broke. During the summer he worked for the Department of Natural Resources and his paycheck helped some in keeping all our bodies and souls together through those never ending hard times. It was Uncle Bud who taught me how to trap and skin the critters I caught, which allowed me to have some extra spendin' money for important stuff like shotgun and rifle shells and a new fishing lure now and then. And nearly every Sunday afternoon in the winter he'd take me along with him to Eagle River to watch the Eagle River Northernaires play hockey. I loved hockey.

So, I decided to take on a project that would change Uncle Bud's mind about goin' with Dad and the gang to Devine Lake for our Annual Duck Hunting and Camping Outing. And I knew I could do it too!

As I saw it, the major obstacle standing in my way was the lack of a 12 gauge shotgun for Uncle Bud to use while huntin' those ducks. If I could somehow come up with one, I was sure he's soften up and come with us. After all, he did hunt ducks with us for a couple of years and seemed to have a good time, just like the rest of us.

After givin' my idea a chance to bounce around in my brain for a few minutes I suddenly remembered where I could find that 12 gauge I needed to cement my plan. And I just knew the guy who owned it wouldn't even think twice about letting Uncle Bud borrow it. The guy was one of our duck huntin' gang,...Charlie!

Back in the Dark Ages, when I was a kid, hardly anybody owned TWO SHOTGUNS! Only really rich people could afford more than one shotgun, and I didn't know any rich people. At least not any that lived in the north woods. Lots of those summer tourists were rich, but they probably didn't hunt ducks anyway. But even though Charlie wasn't rich, he owned two shotguns!

When Charlie and his wife moved north from Chicago, among their possessions was an ancient double barreled shotgun. The name of the manufacturer escapes my memory, but it was old, and it still fired. Charlie had used it a few times when Dad was trying to teaching him how to hunt grouse. But when Dad decided to trade in his old LaFever side by side for a new, modern Remington Model 870 pump gun, Charlie followed suit. Only he didn't trade in his old double. At the time I didn't know why, (and I still don't know why he didn't!)

I told Dad about my plan and he said he thought it'd work. So we drove over to Charlie's house to ask the question. After a short explanation as to why we wanted to borrow his old double, Charlie wasted no time in saying "Heck yes!" Charlie, like everybody who knew Uncle Bud, liked him a lot. Also, Charlie was excited to have Uncle Bud along on our duck hunting adventure, as the two of them would probably team up and hunt together. Charlie liked the idea of having a hunting partner for the upcoming duck season opener. Now I was sure Uncle Bud would agree to come along with us. And I was right!

Opening morning found four eager duck hunters setting up camp on the northeast side of the island in the middle of Devine Lake. Shooting time on opening day started at noon, so we hurried to get our campsite ship shape by eleven o'clock. And by shortly before eleven our home away from home was all in order and our canoes were loaded with duck hunting gear, ready to depart.

As usual, Dad and I headed east, where our blind overlooked a large patch of open water at the mouth of a small spring creek that lazily contributed it's clear, cold waters into Devine Lake. Most of the lake was covered with thick stands of wild rice, so it was necessary to find a location with some open area in which hunters could place their decoys. The lake bottom, at this point, contained a thick layer of stinky, black muck. Our decoys had to be placed and picked up with the aid of our canoe. But the extra work was worth it, because ducks loved to visit this area.

On the other hand, Charlie and Uncle Bud opted to head northwest, to a location Dad had dubbed "No Ducks Point". Here the rice was sparse, and usually few duck ventured there. But the lake bottom was solid, comprised of gravel and sand, making it easy to wade out and place your decoys, and do the same when it was time to pick them up at day's end. By 11:45 a.m. all was ready. We now only had to wait for the ducks. In less than a half hour our wait was over.

At the magical hour of noon, from hundreds of pot holes, rivers and lakes throughout the surrounding area, the harvest began. Flock after flock of mallards, black ducks, blue winged teal and ring necked ducks descended on Devine Lake. Filled with such a magnificent stand of wild rice, it was a duck magnet! Even if one wasn't a duck hunter, just watching such an awe inspiring spectacle would have been well worth the price of admission!

Throughout the afternoon Dad and I thumped away at incoming birds at a fairly consistent pace. By 2:30 p.m. Dad had easily filled his limit of plump, rice fattened mallards and black ducks. It took his hunting companion a little longer to do likewise. With our limits filled, we simply sat in our blind, relaxed, and watched the rest of the show. It was time well spent!

Memories of those peaceful fall afternoons, the sound of wind rushing over cupped wings, hundreds of ducks silhouetted against a deep blue October sky, plus the overpowering smells of fall, are memories that will endure till my final breath! The shooting of a few ducks is but a minor reason for spending time in such a magnificent setting, such as the one Mother Nature created in Devine Lake.

As the afternoon deepened, Dad, Old Pat and I lay back in the deep, soft, marsh grass and listened to the sounds of a duck marsh on opening day. From a half dozen other duck blinds scattered around Devine Lake came occasional bursts of shotgun fire, as ducks continued to provide the hunters with plump targets. But from the direction of "No Ducks Point", all was quiet. Dad and I had heard a couple of shots shortly after the opening hour, but since then, only silence. Very strange. But then again, the spot was well named.

By 5:00 p.m., our limits filled, and still over an hour of legal shooting time remaining, Dad and I picked up our decoys and paddled to our campsite. We were surprised to see Charlie's canoe pulled up on the shore and a thin column of smoke curling lazily skyward from our campfire pit. Charlie and Uncle Bud were sitting on opposite sides of the fire, mute as clothing store dummies. Dad looked at me and whispered, "Oh, oh, this don't look good." And as usual, Dad was right!

Without trying to look like a couple of show offs, we deposited our armloads of ducks in a heap nest to our tent and Dad cheerfully asked, "Well, how'd you guys do?" It was almost like the lid came off Pandora's Box!

For a few seconds neither Charlie nor Uncle Bud said anything. It was like each of them were waiting for the other one to answer. Charlie broke the silence.

"Well,...er,...ah,...ahem,...Bud had a little unfortunate accident".

Uncle Bud didn't quite agree with Charlie's diagnosis. "ACCIDENT MY (bleep)! CHARLIE, YOU KNOW (bleep) WELL, THAT WAS NO ACCIDENT! YOU CONFESSED TO ME AFTERWARDS THAT (bleeping) OLD DOUBLE BARREL OF YOURS ALWAYS DID THAT!!! I could tell right off that Uncle Bud wasn't happy.

Charlie hunkered down into a defensive posture. "Well,...ah,...er,...ahem,...I don't think I said it ALWAYS did that, I think I said it did it SOMETIMES."

Uncle Bud's memory of the incident was slightly different. "YOU'RE FULL OF (bleep)! YOU TOLD ME IT ALWAYS DID THAT!!". Besides the smoke from our campfire, there were also wisps of smoke curling out of Uncle Bud's ears! He was hot! Charlie's face was pale.

Dad assumed the role of referee, and with his voice raised slightly commanded, "Hey, hey, cool down, both of you! What in the (bleep) happened? What are you two yelling at each other about?"

Uncle Bud rolled up his sleeve on his right arm and pointed to his biceps. It was slightly swollen and radiated the color of purple grapes. "THAT'S WHAT HAPPENED!", yelled a crimson faced Uncle Bud, as a few more puffs of smoke came sifting out from under his cap.

Dad and I looked at each other with puzzled looks on our faces. We still had no idea of what hat happened to Uncle Bud which turned his biceps purple, and had started a war of verbal outbursts.

Charlie explained. "Shortly after noon, a duck swung over our decoys. I took aim and shot, and knocked the bird down. But it only had a broken wing and started swimming along the bank, heading for a clump of rice. Bud jumped out of our blind and ran down the shore to finish the cripple off before it got away. He pulled up,....aimed, and,...." Before Charlie could finish the story, Uncle Bud jumped to his feet and supplied the ending.

"WHEN I PULLED THE TRIGGER, NOTHING HAPPENED. I STARTED TO LOWER THE GUN, TRYING TO FIGURE OUT WHY IT DIDN'T GO OFF, AND THEN BOTH BARRELS FIRED! IT KICKED THE (bleeping, bleep) OUT OF MY ARM!"

Uncle Bud had been the victim of a condition known as "hang fire". Old guns with worn parts, or even newer guns with extremely dirty mechanisms, will sometimes have a delayed firing sequence. It is a very dangerous situation indeed.

Now it was Charlie's turn again. "Good thing the water was shallow and the bottom is hard. At least I got my gun back after Bud heaved it into the lake."

Uncle Bud had a suggestion. "GIVE IT BACK TO ME AND I'LL FIND A LOT DEEPER SPOT!"

At this point I had to walk behind the tent, as it was impossible for me to conceal the fact that I considered the events which had just been revealed to us contained a considerable amount of mirth. Even though I knew the recoil of two 12 gauge shotgun shell detonating simultaneously would feel like a mule had kicked you with two feet, the image conjured up in my brain nearly made me bust out loud with laughter. But with Uncle Bud in his present mood, well,... had I laughed in his presence, my life expectancy could have been shortened considerably.

After we cleaned our ducks, ate supper, and the adults had sipped a couple of small nightcaps, camp camaraderie returned to near normal. Even Uncle Bud got a few snickers out of his experience, once he had retold his gruesome tale several times. And of course, each new verbal account added additional adjectives to the telling of his ordeal.

The next morning, when our alarm clock dragged us out of our sleeping bags, Uncle Bud informed us that he was going to skip the duck hunting and sleep in. As I recall, he had one additional question for his hunting companion, just as Charlie was preparing to depart for his blind on "No Ducks Point".

"Hey Charlie, just where did you hide that old double barrel?"

# Senior Week, 1955

My God! Where has the time gone??????? Wasn't it just a couple of years ago that I was a freckled faced, snot nosed kid who still believed in Santa Claus, the Easter Bunny and the Tooth Fairy???? Wasn't it just yesterday that I was a terrified freshman, entering Eagle River High School???????? Well anyway, as Dad said, "Time flies when you're havin' fun!" It was hard to believe that here it was, the last week of May, 1955 and I'm nearly graduated from high school! But what a week it was!

Me and high school, (ah, make that "high school and I") got along real fine. I really liked school. I got along just fine with most all the kids that went to high school, and continued a wonderful friendship with the seven I had spent eight years with in the St. Germain Grade School. I can't remember a single teacher I didn't like. Well, a couple were "so-so", but all in all my school years were great years and provide me with some super memories. I'm not sure I'd like to go back in time and do it all over again. Maybe for a few of the parties and baseball games, but not the whole twelve years. But then again,...no, forget it, not the whole twelve years!

Going to school was a lit different back in the 40's and 50's than it is today. But of course, what isn't different than it was in the 40's and 50's? Not much. One nice thing about going to school back in the old days was that the teachers were in charge. The school officials had the authority to actually DISCIPLINE students who violated the rules and regulations. If you screwed up and busted the rules, you got busted. Maybe with a yard stick on your behind, or a swift kick in the rear, or in some cases, a leather belt on the backside. For lesser felonies, maybe a good twist of the ear or a simple shaking up might be your punishment.

Believe me, I speak from first hand experience, these were excellent behavior modifiers and tremendous character builders. I received my share of the above mentioned reactions due to my occasional poor judgment when making choices. And there is no doubt in my mind that the strict and immediate justice system used when I went to school made me a better person. And needless to say, greatly improved my ability to make better positive choices.

And to end my ramblings on this subject, whenever I received punishment in school, I had it coming. Believe me, I had it coming!

Eagle River High School was a neat place. The total enrollment in grades nine through twelve was about two hundred and twenty five students. The senior class of '55 contained fifty three graduating seniors. What was nice about ERHS, a student could get a really good education, if they wanted to. Plus, if you obeyed the rules, or at least were careful enough, or lucky enough, to not get caught bending the rules a tad, you could have a really fun time while you were getting educated. I guess one might call a situation like that, "the best of two worlds".

In order for the reader to realize how "Senior Week" worked out so great for myself and a batch of my buddies and friends, you'll have to understand how the grading system worked at good old ERHS. And, how the grading system offered a tremendous reward for those students who put in some extra effort. Effort that REALLY paid off during "Senior Week".

When report card time rolled around each quarter, the teachers computed your quarter grade by adding up all your recorded scores on homework, tests, and et. to arrive at a PRECISE percentage. If you were the class brain, your report card grade in "Algebra" might be "99". If you were the class clown, your report card grade in "Single Digit Math" might be "39". Any grade below "75" and you "flunked". The system inspired most students to avoid being the class clown.

Now comes the good part. If a senior maintained a yearly average of "90" or above in a specific subject, YOU DIDN'T HAVE TO TAKE A "FINAL EXAM" IN THAT SUBJECT!!!! Now that's what a rabbit would call a mighty big carrot! And,...during "Final Exam Week", seniors who were exempt from taking an exam did not even have to be in the school building during that exam's time slot! WOW! That was a whole semi-truck load of carrots!

Well, in the case of yours truly, I was wise enough to keep my nose in the books deep enough to escape finals in Chemistry, U.S. History, Advanced Math, and Advanced Typing. But, by ending up with an average of "89" in my foreign language class, I had to take a final exam. My foreign language class was called "English IV".

But, all in all, only having to take one Final in a whole week of school didn't shape up to be a rotten carrot. Most of my friends and buddies were all in about the same situation. A handful of disgusting "brains" had the whole week off!

On Friday, preceding "Senior Week", our iron fisted principal, Mr. Kracht, posted the "Senior's Final Testing Schedule" on the school's bulletin board. And let me tell you, it didn't take long for Tom Dean, Hank Maines and Yours Truly to hatch up a spectacular plan for our final week as Seniors!

As we rode home on our bus that wonderful Friday afternoon, our bold plan took shape. The first step would be most difficult. First we'd have to convince our parents that our plan was safe and sensible, and being such model students (choke, choke) we would also deserve such a reward. The second step would be to talk one of our parents into allowing us to use their car for a full week. If those two hurdles could be overcome, the rest would be a cakewalk!

Here was our master plan. We'd camp out somewhere in the virgin wilderness along Plum Crick. That way we could come and go as we pleased and our parents would never find out how late we stayed out for all the parties that were being planned by ourselves and our classmates. Also, during those long periods when we were not required to be in the school building, we could do all the trout fishing we wanted to do. Why we'd feast on those succulent, pink meat brook trout three meals a day. And hundreds of those speckled beauties inhabited the icy cold waters of Plum Crick. We'd be "Kings for a Week".

All three of us met with all three pairs of our parents and "sweet talked" them into letting us plan on camping out for our final week of high school. We did a masterful job of being the perfect, polished diplomats, using lines like, "We just want to get away from all the pressure of Senior Week", and "Wouldn't an outing like this be a nice reward for how well we all did in school?" and several other assorted bits or hogwash and teenage deception. Well, we had no trouble completing Step One.

And much to my surprise, my Dad and Mom volunteered to let us use their big, black, impressive looking '49 Buick Super to fill our transportation needs. We were in business!

We knew just the spot to set up our base of operations. A tiny two rut abandoned logging road forked west off Plum Creek Avenue and led to a high hill overlooking the fabled Plum Crick. The crest of the hill was flat and nicely protected by the crowns of a dozen or so mature jack pine trees. It was without a doubt a splendid camping spot! We could probably have camped there all summer and not a soul would have discovered our whereabouts. Such are the dreams of youth.

Tom and I were both eighteen, and Hank a year younger. So, it was fairly simple for us to stock up on our most desired staple. Beer! Vilas County had an abundance of "beer bars" which at the time could legally sell "The brew that made Milwaukee famous" to eighteen year olds. The six cases we purchased stacked nicely in one corner of our tent. And the icy stream that flowed below our camping spot made a perfect beer cooler.

We added a few more necessary items which any well stocked camp needs. We bought bread, a few dozen eggs, bacon, a bag of flour to coat all those trout we were going to catch, some peanut butter and jelly, a few candy bars and bags of potato chips, etc., etc. When Monday rolled around we were primed and ready for "Senior Week"!

Ah, and what a week it was! Thinking back, I guess it was the first time in any of our lives that we realized how truly wonderful it was to be in complete and total control of our lives.

Why, we could do nearly anything we wanted to do. We could cruise around town in that long, black, sleek, Buick, looking as cool and any teenager looked in the 50's. Or, we might just lollygag on the lawn in front of our high school and torment the students who were inside that were being forced to spar with Final Exams. Or, we could pick up some chicks and go for a little ride in the country and plot yet another party. Then again, we might opt to go for a quick dip in Silver Lake, which was just a hop, skip and a jump down the street from good old ERHS, Or, well, you get the point. We were what might be thought of as "Cool Dudes". At least in our own minds.

The week sped along, as all good times do, and we made every effort to cram all the excitement we could into every second. And we did a dang good job of it too!

We did catch a few pan sized brook trout to dine on, but to be honest, the earlier talk of doing "lot's of trout fishing" kind of fizzled out. Once we got into the swing of Senior Week, the trout fishing seemed all too tame. We partied often, but with caution and some small bits of restraint, not causing anyone any harm nor reaching a condition which might have put us in harms way. Or possibly not being able to find our way back to our campsite. And then again, maybe a couple of times we were just plain lucky. Such is youth.

By mid week we were forced to spend a little time back at our homes to allow our parents to check us out and be reassured we hadn't fled the country or be listed on the nations "Top Most Ten Wanted". Also, we needed a good shower and some clean clothing, along with a raid on our parent's kitchens to replenish our dwindling food reserves. Our supply of Milwaukee Suds was still holding out fairly well. Boy, were we lucky our parents would never find out about that little secret! Such are the dreams of youth.

All in all, things were working out just great. Our home in the woods was Dad's big umbrella tent he and I always used on our camping trips. Tom and Hank even got fairly used to the musty smell after a couple of days.

There was plenty of room for the three of us, plus our supplies. Tom had his sleeping bad against the north wall of the tent and mine occupied the south wall. Hank had selected the center of the floor for his sleeping area. Actually it didn't matter where we decided to bed down, as the location we had chosen was perfectly flat, with good drainage away from the tent in case it might rain. The weather had remained unseasonably sunny and warm. The view of Plum Creek right below us and the calming gurgle of it's waters made our camping spot rate an eleven on a scale of one to ten. And the peace and quiet allowed us to sleep like babies. At least for a few hours each night. That is, up until Thursday.

We had slipped back into our camp shortly after midnight, a short time after evening party number four had ended. Sleep came quickly,...and so did the rain. Lots of rain. Hard driving rain. With thunder and lightning!

Tom and I were dragged out of our fitful sleep somewhere around two thirty by a whimpering plea from Hank. Actually is was more like a bold announcement rather than a whimper, but later when Tom and I told the story to our friends, we decided the word "whimpering" sounded better than "screamed".

"HEY!, I believe is how Hank began his declaration. "I'M SOAKING WET AND FREEZING TO DEATH!"

Tom flipped on his flashlight to reveal Hank and his sleeping bag partially immersed in water. The "totally flat" location where we erected our tent actually turned out to be "totally concave". And Hank was resting in the lowest portion of the depression. The rainwater had seeped it's way under our tent and then seeped it's through the canvas floor. Tom and I felt sorry for our companion, but not sorry enough to comply with his next request.

"I'm really cold. Would one of you let me crawl in your sleeping bag and sleep with you?"

A wave of horror passed through Tom's and my minds as we rapidly digested Hank's request. My first reaction was, "Hank, you must be out of your mind!" Tom was less gentle. "Jeeessss, Hank, what do you think we are, a couple of homos?"

Our minds quickly considered what out buddies and classmates would think if they heard two guys had spent the night together in a tent, and in THE SAME SLEEPING BAG! What our buddies and classmates would SAY about such a situation was even more frightening! Tom and I had a better suggestion for our dear friend.

"Go sleep in the back seat of the car. Cover up with a towel or something! And so poor Hank crawled into the back seat of my parent's Buick and shivered his way till dawn. After we got our morning campfire going Hank thawed out in less than an hour.

The final day of Senior Week melted into history and the trio of campers took down the tent, packed our gear and I drove them to their respective homes. We were happy, but tired, and no doubt none the wiser. Such is youth.

Graduation took place the next week and our four eventful, fun filled years at good old ERHS came to a conclusion. Another chapter in our lives had been completed. The summer of '55 loomed ahead.

Several week after Senior Week had passed, Dad and I found some time to be together and just do some talking. I was fond of those sessions. So was Dad. Our conversation somehow got around to "What did you three REALLY do while camping out during Senior Week?"

I knew that Dad knew we weren't lily white about our original intentions as they were outlined to our parents when we first launched our plan. Dad had been a teenage male once upon a time, and he had a good memory. And Dad was impossible to lie to. So, without too many SPECIFIC details, I filled him in on SOME of our experiences, which I hoped would be enough information to put the lid on this subject for all times. And at first I thought I had been successful.

When I ended my edited story of what Tom, Hank and I had been doing during our week away from home, Dad had a final comment.

"Ya", he began, "I took a little trout fishing trip to Plum Creek the week you three were camped out there."

My stomach began to twitch.

"Nice spot you guys picked for your camp."

The twitch became a knot.

"Nice bunch of supplies you had piled in in one corner of your tent."

I began looking for an escape route.

But that was the end of Dad's comments. He just grinned at me with his friendly, all knowing, grin on his face and walked away.

I guess he figured his kid had finally growed up. Ah,...make that grown up.

# About The Author

Being born and raised during the toughest of times created by the Great Depression, subsisting in rural America challenged millions of its citizens. "Buckshot" and his family, using innovative skills and hard work, survived. And they grew stronger because of the challenge. "Dad" and "Mom" Anderson allowed their only child to become a partner in helping to keep the wolf away from their cabin door. The lessons he learned helped him finish college and serve 36 distinguished years in public education. In addition, his summer job guiding fishermen, has earned him an induction into the National Freshwater Fishing Hall of Fame as a "Legendary Guide". But during his formative years he learned, "Growing up isn't ALL Fishing and Hunting".

Printed in the United States
1187200002B/404-572